Marx Joyce
Hardy Austen
Defoe Melville Hugo
Eliot
Stoker Molière
Wilde Maupassant Byron
Garnett Engels Schiller
Goethe Hawthorne Kafka
Cotton Dostoyevsky
Baum Kipling Doyle
Henry Nietzsche
Flaubert Turgenev Balzac
Stockton Vatsyayana Crane
Burroughs Verne
Curtis Tocqueville Vinci
Homer Tolstoy Busch
Darwin Thoreau
Potter Zola Twain
Lawrence
Kant Jowett Stevenson Dickens
Andersen
London Descartes
Poe Aristotle Wells
Hale James Hastings
Bunner Shakespeare Cooke
Richter Chambers Irving
Doré Benedict Alcott
Pushkin
Newton

Abbott Machiavelli Montaigne Chesterton Cooper Emerson Haggard Grimm Carroll Christie Einstein Fitzgerald Smith Hall Willis Leslie Dumas Whitman Gogol Widger Freud Plato Scott Cervantes Burton Hesse Harte Voltaire Chekhov da Shaw Wodehouse Dante Swift

tredition®

tredition was established in 2006 by Sandra Latusseck and Soenke Schulz. Based in Hamburg, Germany, tredition offers publishing solutions to authors and publishing houses, combined with worldwide distribution of printed and digital book content. tredition is uniquely positioned to enable authors and publishing houses to create books on their own terms and without conventional manufacturing risks.

For more information please visit: www.tredition.com

TREDITION CLASSICS

This book is part of the TREDITION CLASSICS series. The creators of this series are united by passion for literature and driven by the intention of making all public domain books available in printed format again - worldwide. Most TREDITION CLASSICS titles have been out of print and off the bookstore shelves for decades. At tredition we believe that a great book never goes out of style and that its value is eternal. Several mostly non-profit literature projects provide content to tredition. To support their good work, tredition donates a portion of the proceeds from each sold copy. As a reader of a TREDITION CLASSICS book, you support our mission to save many of the amazing works of world literature from oblivion. See all available books at www.tredition.com.

Project Gutenberg

The content for this book has been graciously provided by Project Gutenberg. Project Gutenberg is a non-profit organization founded by Michael Hart in 1971 at the University of Illinois. The mission of Project Gutenberg is simple: To encourage the creation and distribution of eBooks. Project Gutenberg is the first and largest collection of public domain eBooks.

The Adventures of Daniel Boone: the Kentucky rifleman

Francis L. (Francis Lister) Hawks

Imprint

This book is part of TREDITION CLASSICS

Author: Francis L. (Francis Lister) Hawks
Cover design: Buchgut, Berlin – Germany

Publisher: tredition GmbH, Hamburg - Germany
ISBN: 978-3-8472-1586-8

www.tredition.com
www.tredition.de

The intention of the TREDITION CLASSICS series is to make world literature in the public domain available in printed format. Literary enthusiasts and organizations, such as Project Gutenberg, worldwide have scanned and digitally edited the original texts. tredition has subsequently formatted and redesigned the content into a modern reading layout. Therefore, we cannot guarantee the exact reproduction of the original format of a particular historic edition. Please also note that no modifications have been made to the spelling, therefore it may differ from the orthography used today.

[Pg 1]
[Pg 2]
[Pg 4]
[Pg 3]

DANIEL BOON. From the Basso Relievo in the Rotunda of the Capitol at Washington

THE

ADVENTURES

OF

DANIEL BOONE,

THE

KENTUCKY RIFLEMAN.

BY
THE AUTHOR OF "UNCLE PHILIP'S CONVERSATIONS."

"Too much crowded—too much crowded—I want more elbow-room."—*Boone on his way to Missouri.*

NEW YORK:
D. APPLETON & CO., 200 BROADWAY.
PHILADELPHIA:
GEORGE S. APPLETON, 164 CHESNUT ST.

MDCCCL.

~~~~~~

TO
HIS YOUNG COUNTRYMEN
THROUGHOUT THE UNITED STATES,
AND ESPECIALLY
THE LADS OF KENTUCKY,

This Volume
IS AFFECTIONATELY DEDICATED,

By Uncle Philip.

[Pg 8]
[Pg 9]
~~~~~~

THE

ADVENTURES OF DANIEL BOONE.

CHAPTER I.

SOME men choose to live in crowded cities;—others are pleased with the peaceful quiet of a country farm; while some love to roam through wild forests, and make their homes in the wilderness. The man of whom I shall now speak, was one of this last class. Perhaps you never heard of Daniel Boone, the Kentucky rifleman. If not, then I have a strange and interesting story to tell you.

If, when a child was born, we knew that he was to become a remarkable man, the time and place of his birth would, perhaps, be always remembered. But as this can not be known, great mistakes are often made on these points. As to the time when Daniel Boone [Pg 14] was born, there is no difficulty; but people have fallen into many blunders about the place. Some have said that he was born in England, before his parents left that country; others that he came into this world during the passage of his parents across the Atlantic. One has told us that he was born in Virginia; another in Maryland; while many have stated that he was a native of North Carolina. These are all mistakes. Daniel Boone was born in the year 1746, in Bucks county, in the state of Pennsylvania.

From some cause or other, when the boy was but three years old, his parents moved from this home, and settled upon the Schuylkill river, not far from the town of Reading. Here they lived for ten years; and it was during this time that their son Daniel began to show his passion for hunting. He was scarcely able to carry a gun, when he was shooting all the squirrels, rackoons, and even wild-cats (it is said), that he could find in that region. As he grew older, his courage increased, and then we find him amusing himself with higher game. Other lads in the neighborhood were soon taught by him the use of the rifle, and were then able to join him in his adventures. On one occasion, they all started out for a hunt, and after amusing themselves till it was almost dark, were returning homeward, when suddenly a wild cry was heard in the woods. The boys screamed out, [Pg 15] "A panther! a panther!" and ran off as fast as they could. Boone stood firmly, looking around for the animal. It was a panther indeed. His eye lighted upon him just in the act of springing toward him: in an instant he levelled his rifle, and shot him through the heart.

But this sort of sport was not enough for him. He seemed resolved to go away from men, and live in the forests with these animals. One morning he started off as usual, with his rifle and dog. Night came on, but Daniel did not return to his home. Another day and night passed away, and still the boy did not make his appearance. His parents were now greatly alarmed. The neighbors joined them in making search for the lad. After wandering about a great while, they at length saw smoke rising from a cabin in the distance. Upon reaching it, they found the boy. The floor of the cabin was covered with the skins of such animals as he had slain, and pieces of meat were roasting before the fire for his supper. Here, at a distance of three miles from any settlement, he had built his cabin of sods and branches, and sheltered himself in the wilderness.

It was while his father was living on the head-waters of the Schuylkill, that young Boone received, so far as we know, all his education. Short indeed were his schoolboy days. It happened that an Irish schoolmaster strolled into the settlement, [Pg 16] and, by the advice of Mr. Boone and other parents, opened a school in the neighborhood. It was not then as it is now. Good schoolhouses were not scattered over the land; nor were schoolmasters always able to teach their pupils. The schoolhouse where the boys of this settlement went was a log cabin, built in the midst of the woods. The schoolmaster was a strange man: sometimes good-humored, and then indulging the lads; sometimes surly and ill-natured, and then beating them severely. It was his usual custom, after hearing the first lessons of the morning, to allow the children to be out for a half hour at play, during which time he strolled off to refresh himself from his labors. He always walked in the same direction, and the boys thought that after his return, when they were called in, he was generally more cruel than ever. They were whipped more severely, and, oftentimes without any cause. They observed this, but did not know the meaning of it. One morning young Boone asked that he might go out, and had scarcely left the schoolroom, when he saw a squirrel running over the trunk of a fallen tree. True to his nature, he instantly gave chase, until at last the squirrel darted into a bower of vines and branches. Boone thrust his hand in, and, to his surprise, laid of hold of a bottle of whiskey. This was in the direction of his master's morning walks, and he thought now that he understood the secret of [Pg 17] much of his ill-nature. He returned to the schoolroom; but when they were dismissed for that day, he told some of the larger boys of his discovery. Their plan was soon arranged. Early the next morning a bottle of whiskey, having tartar emetic in it, was placed in the bower, and the other bottle thrown away. At the usual hour, the lads were sent out to play, and the master started on his walk. But their play was to come afterward: they longed for the master to return. At length they were called in, and in a little time saw the success of their experiment. The master began to look pale and sick, yet still went on with his work. Several boys were called up, one after the other, to recite lessons, and all whipped soundly, whether right or wrong. At last young Boone was called out to answer questions in arithmetic. He came forward with his slate and pencil, and the master began: "If you subtract six from nine, what remains?" said he. "Three, sir," said Boone. "Very good," said the master; "now let us come to fractions. If you take three quarters from a whole number, what remains?"—"The whole, sir," answered Boone. "You blockhead!" cried the master, beating him, "you stupid little fool, how can you show that?"—"If I take one bottle of whiskey," said Boone, "and put in its place another in which I have mixed an emetic, the whole will remain, if nobody drinks it!" The [Pg 18] Irishman, dreadfully sick, was now doubly enraged. He seized Boone, and commenced beating him: the children shouted and roared; the scuffle continued, until Boone knocked the master down upon the floor, and rushed out of the room. It was a day of freedom now for the lads. The story soon ran through the neighborhood; Boone was rebuked by his parents, but the schoolmaster was dismissed, and thus ended the boy's education.

Thus freed from school, he now returned more ardently than ever to his favorite pursuit. His dog and rifle were his constant companions, and day after day he started from home, only to roam through the forests. Hunting seemed to be the only business of his life; and he was never so happy as when at night he came home laden with game. He was an untiring wanderer.

I do not know but that this passion for roaming was in some degree inherited by Daniel Boone. His father had already had three homes: one in England, one in Bucks county, and another on the Schuylkill; and he now thought of removing further. It is said that the passion of Daniel for hunting was one cause which prompted his father to think of this. Land was becoming scarce, the neighborhood a little crowded, and game less abundant; and, to mend matters, he began to cast his eyes around for a new home. He was not long in choosing one. He had heard of a rich and [Pg 19] beautiful country on the banks of the Yadkin river in North Carolina, and he determined that this should be the next resting-place for him and his household.

All things were made ready as soon as possible, and the journey commenced. It was a fine spring morning when the father started for his new home, with his wife and children, his flocks and herds. Their journey lay hundreds of miles through a trackless wilderness; yet with cheerful and fearless hearts they pressed onward. When hungry, they feasted upon venison and wild turkeys (for Daniel, with his rifle, was in company); when thirsty, they found cool springs of water to refresh them by the way; when wearied at night, they laid themselves down and slept under the wide-spreading branches of the forest. At length they reached the land they looked for, and the father found it to be all that he expected. The woods in that region were unbroken; no man seemed yet to have found them. Land was soon cleared, a cabin built, and the father in a little time found himself once more happily settled with his family.

The old man with his other sons went busily to the work of making a farm. As for Daniel, they knew it was idle to expect his help in such employment, and therefore left him to roam about with his rifle. This was a glorious country for the youth; wild woods were all around him, and the game, [Pg 20] having not yet learned to fear the crack of the rifle wandered fearlessly through them. This he thought was, of all places, the home for him. I hope you will not think that he was the idle and useless boy of the family, for it was not so. While the farm was improving, Daniel was supplying the family with provisions. The table at home was always filled with game, and they had enough and to spare. Their house became known as a warm-hearted and hospitable abode; for the wayfaring wanderer, when lost in the woods, was sure to find here a welcome, a shelter, and an abundance. Then, too, if money was wanted in the family, the peltries of the animals shot by Daniel supplied it: so that he was, in a large degree, the supporter of the household. In this way years rolled onward—the farm still enlarging and improving, Daniel still hunting, and the home one of constant peace, happiness, and plenty.

At length the story of the success and comfort of the family brought neighbors around them. Different parts of the forests began to be cleared; smoke was soon seen rising from new cabins; and the sharp crack of other rifles than Daniel's was sometimes heard in the morning. This grieved him sadly. Most people would have been pleased to find neighbors in the loneliness of the woods; but what pleased others did not please him. They were crowding upon him; they were driving away [Pg 21] his game: this was his trouble. But, after all, there was one good farmer who came into the region and made his settlement; which settlement, as it turned out, proved a happy thing for Daniel. This was a very worthy man named Bryan. He cleared his land, built his cabin upon a sloping hill, not very far from Mr. Boone's, and before a great while, by dint of industry, had a good farm of more than a hundred acres. This farm was beautifully situated. A pretty stream of water almost encircled it. On the banks of the Schuylkill, Daniel Boone found all his education, such as it was; on the banks of the Yadkin he found something far better. I must tell you now of a very strange adventure.

One evening, with another young friend, he started out upon what is called a "*fire-hunt*." Perhaps you do not know what this means. I will explain it to you. Two people are always necessary for a fire-hunt. One goes before, carrying a blazing torch of pitch-pine wood (or lightwood, as it is called in the southern country), while the other follows behind with his rifle. In this way the two hunters move through the forests. When an animal is startled, he will stand gazing at the light, and his eyes may be seen shining distinctly: this is called "*shining the eyes*." The hunter with the rifle, thus seeing him, while the other *shines* him, levels his gun with steady aim, and has a fair shot. [Pg 22] This mode of hunting is still practised in many parts of our country, and is everywhere known as a *fire-hunt*.

Boone, with his companion, started out upon such a hunt, and very soon reached the woods skirting the lower end of Mr. Bryan's farm. It seems they were on horseback, Boone being behind with the rifle. They had not gone far, when his companion reined up his horse, and two eyes were seen distinctly shining. Boone levelled his rifle, but something prevented his firing. The animal darted off. Boone leaped from his horse, left his companion, and instantly dashed after it. It was too dark to see plainly, still he pursued; he was close upon its track, when a fence coming in the way, the animal leaped it with a clear bound. Boone climbed over as fast as he could with his rifle, but the game had got ahead. Nothing daunted by this, he pushed on, until he found himself at last not very far from Mr. Bryan's home. But the animal was gone. It was a strange chase. He determined to go into Mr Bryan's house, and tell his adventure. As he drew near, the dogs raised a loud barking, the master came out, bade him welcome, and carried him into the house. Mr. Bryan had scarcely introduced him to his family as "the son of his neighbor Boone," when suddenly the door of the room was burst open, and in rushed a little lad of seven, followed by a girl of sixteen years, crying [Pg 23] out, "O father! father! sister is frightened to death! She went down to the river, and was chased by a panther!" The hunter and his game had met. There stood Boone, leaning upon his rifle, and Rebecca Bryan before him, gasping for breath. From that moment he continued to pursue it; Farmer Bryan's house became a favorite resort for him; he loved it as well as the woods. The business was now changed: Rebecca Bryan completely *shined his eyes*; and after a time, to the great joy of themselves and both families, Daniel Boone and Rebecca Bryan were married. It proved, as you will see, a very happy marriage to both parties.

Being now a married man, it became Daniel Boone's duty to seek a new home for himself. In a little time, therefore, he left his wife, and wandered into the unsettled parts of North Carolina in search of one. After moving about for some time, he found, upon the headwaters of the Yadkin, a rich soil, covered with a heavy and once more unbroken forest. "Here," thought Daniel Boone, "is the resting-place for me; here Rebecca Bryan and myself may be happy: this shall be our home." He returned to his wife, and she, with a cheerful heart, joined in all his plans. With tears in her eyes, she bade farewell to her friends; yet, with a light spirit, she started off with her husband. A clearing in the woods was [Pg 24] soon made, a log cabin of his own soon built, and a portion of ground planted. Boone seems now to have thought that he must do something more than use his rifle. He was to make a home for his wife and busied himself, accordingly, in enlarging his farm as fast as he could, and industriously cultivating it. Still, on his busiest day, he would find a leisure hour to saunter with his gun to the woods, and was sure never to return without game. His own table was loaded with it, as when at his father's, and his house, like his father's, soon became known as a warm and kind shelter for the wandering traveller. In this industrious and quiet way of farming and hunting, years were spent, and Daniel Boone was contented and happy. Several little children were now added to his group; and, with his wife, his children, and his rifle, for companions, he felt that all was well.

But his peace was at length disturbed once more. His old troubles pursued him; men again began to come near. The crash of falling trees was heard, as the new settlers levelled the forests; huts were seen springing up all around him; other hunters were roaming through the woods, and other dogs than his were heard barking. This was more than he was willing to bear. Happy as he had made his home, he determined to leave it, and find another in the wilderness, where he could have that wilderness to himself. For some time he was [Pg 25] at a loss to know where to go; yet his heart was fixed in the determination to move. The circumstances which pointed him to his new home, and where that new home was made, you may learn in the next chapter. [Pg 26]

CHAPTER II.

MY young friends all know where the state of Kentucky is situated. It is hardly necessary for me to say, that at the time of which I am writing, that region was an unbroken wilderness.

It was in the year 1754 that a white man first visited the country of Kentucky. This was James M'Bride. In company with several others during that year, he was passing down the Ohio, when he discovered the mouth of Kentucky river, and made a landing. Near the spot where he landed, he cut upon a tree the first letters of his name; and these letters, it is said, could be seen and distinctly read for many years afterward. With his companions, he wandered through the wilderness; the country struck them all as being remarkably beautiful. It is not wonderful, then, that when they returned home, they were filled with fine stories [Pg 27] about the new region. They declared that it was "the best tract of land in North America, and probably in the world."

In spite of their pleasant stories, however, it was a long time before any one was disposed to follow in their track. At length, Doctor Walker, of Virginia, with a number of friends, started upon a western tour of discovery. Some say that he was in search of the Ohio river particularly; others that he went merely to collect strange plants and flowers. Be this as it may, he with his party wandered through Powell's Valley, and passed the mountains at what is called the Cumberland Gap. They then crossed the Cumberland river, and roaming on through the forests, at length, after much fatigue and suffering, reached the Big Sandy. The country was beautiful, yet they were too much worn out to go further, and from this point began to return homeward. They had suffered more than M'Bride, and therefore their story was not so bright as his; yet they gave a very pleasant account of the new country.

No one yet, however, seemed ready to make his home in Kentucky; and accident at last seems to have thrown one man into that country, whose story, upon his return, made some anxious to go there. This was John Finley, a backwoodsman of North Carolina. He was in the habit of roving about and trading with the Indians. In the year [Pg 28] 1767, he, with certain companions as fearless as himself, led on from place to place by the course of trade, wandered far into Kentucky. Here he remained for some time. It was a very beautiful, yet, as he learned also, a very dangerous country. No Indian tribe lived there, but all the tribes roamed over it as a hunting-ground. Upon these hunts, the fierce and warlike people would often meet and wage their bloody battles. These fights were so frequent and so awful, that the region was known by the name of the "Dark and Bloody Ground." In spite of danger, Finley lived there, until at last the traders and the Indians began to quarrel, and, for safety's sake, he was forced to run off. He returned to North Carolina, filled with wonderful stories. Sights like those on the "Dark and Bloody Ground," were nowhere to be seen. The land was rich, and covered with trees and flowers; there were lofty mountains, beautiful valleys, and clear streams, throughout it. Then he spoke of the strange caves in the mountains; of curious salt springs; of the footprints of men to be seen distinctly upon the solid rocks; of the strange figures of huge animals on the sides of the high cliffs. Game of all sorts was abundant, from the buffalo down to the partridge. There was no country (he declared) like *Kain-tuck-kee*. [1] [Pg 29] His tale was so wonderful, that people could not well help listening to it.

Whether John Finley was led there by a knowledge of the man's character, or whether it was an accident, it so happened, that about a year after his return, he wandered into the neighborhood of Daniel Boone's home. It was not long before he fell in with Boone, and completely charmed him with his stories. Boone had known some sport in the forests himself, but the adventures of Finley were to him marvellous. He was so much pleased with the man, that he invited him, as it was now winter, to come to his house, and make his home there through the season. The invitation was gladly accepted; and in the cabin of Boone, again and again was the wild beauty of the "Dark and Bloody Ground" laid before him. There was no end to Finley's stories of this region. The wind whistled without, but the fire blazed cheerfully within; and here they sat, on many a night, almost till dawn, Finley talking, and Boone listening. The end of all this was, that they determined, when spring opened, to go to Kentucky. Boone knew that there were hardships and perils in the way, and Finley had practically felt them; but what were dangers or difficulties to these fearless men? The first of May was agreed upon as the day for starting, and Finley was then again to meet Boone at his house. [Pg 30]

It is not strange that other bold men, who heard Finley's stories, were seized with the same desire for going west. Indeed, Boone helped to give them that desire, knowing that a few brave spirits would be of great service in the new country. He talked, therefore, warmly of the comforts of a new home in the forest, where there was an abundance of game, and a complete absence of towns and villages. Accordingly, on the first of May, 1769, when Finley repaired to Boone's house, he found four others ready for the adventure: these were John Stewart, Joseph Holden, James Monay, and William Cool. The people in the neighborhood, learning what was going on, had likewise gathered to look with surprise upon these six men. What could prompt men to leave the comforts of their quiet homes, and wander off into the wilderness? They surely were crazy. Boone was much beloved as a kind neighbor, and they mourned most over his madness. Nothing daunted by all this, they were then ready for a start, and were now on the point of leaving. We are told that, with tears in his eyes, Daniel Boone kissed his wife and children; and if the story be true, I love him the more for it. His spirit was beating for his new hunting-forests; he could face all the dangers of the "Dark and Bloody Ground," but then it was doubtful whether he was not parting with his wife and children for ever. At all events, he was leaving [Pg 31] them for months, perhaps for years—he knew not how long—and who can wonder that tears stood in his eyes? Each man shouldered his rifle, shot-bag, powder-horn, and knapsack, and off they started—every neighbor straining his eyes after them as far as he could see, as the men upon whom he was looking for the last time.

For two or three days they saw nothing new, for they were passing over their old hunting-grounds. After this, they came to a wild and trackless region, and saw from time to time the lofty ridge of mountains which separated them from the western country. In two days more, the provisions with which they had started gave out, and the first thing to be done was to find a fresh supply. Accordingly they halted, chose a suitable spot for their camp, and part of them commenced building it of logs and branches; the others went into the woods in search of game. It was impossible for such men to starve in such a region; game was abundant. The hunters returned toward night, with several deer and wild turkeys. The camp was finished, a bright fire was burning, and in a little time the venison was dressed, cooked, and eaten. The supper was scarcely finished, when they saw dark clouds gathering, and presently they were visited by a tremendous thunder-storm. The sharp lightning flashed through the woods, and the rain poured down in torrents; yet, in their camp they fearlessly sheltered [Pg 32] themselves, the branches covering them from the rain. A man can scarcely be placed during a thunder-storm in a more dangerous place than a forest: every tree is a mark for the lightning; yet these men were calm and self-possessed, and were mercifully protected.

The storm having passed over, they made their arrangements for the night. For safety's sake, two men were to keep a constant watch, while the others slept; and in this duty of watching, they were to take turns. About midnight, while Boone and Holden were keeping the watch, a sharp shrill cry was heard in the woods. They sprang to their feet. "What noise is that?" said Holden. The sound was familiar to Boone. "Be still," said he; "it is only a panther; come along with me." Moving cautiously from the camp, they listened again for the cry. Once more they heard it. Creeping through the woods in the direction of the sound, they at length saw through the darkness the wild, glaring eyes of the animal. Boone levelled his rifle with steady aim, and fired. With a wild yell the panther fell to the ground, and began to retreat. Both were satisfied that the ball had struck him, and returned again to the camp. The crack of the rifle had waked their companions; the adventure was made known to them, and they went quietly to sleep again, satisfied that for the rest of the night at least that panther would not disturb them. [Pg 33]

The next day was a very busy one. Finding game so plenty in the neighborhood, they determined to lay in a good supply. Part of them were therefore out in the woods, hunting, while the rest were in the camp, smoking, drying, and packing the venison for the journey. Fatigued with these labors, when night came they gladly laid themselves down, and, like wearied men, slept soundly.

By the first ray of the morning's light the camp was stirring. Shouldering their rifles and knapsacks, they started on their way. In a little time they found a dead panther. Boone declared that this was his panther; the animal was killed with one ball, and by comparing that ball with those in his shot-bag, he found they were of the same size. In two or three days they reached the foot of the mountains, and began to ascend. Their journey was now rough and wearisome, and they made slow progress. To any men but these, the mountains might have proved impassable; but they were bent upon finding the new hunting-grounds of Kentucky, and nothing could keep them back. After climbing the hills day after day, they found once more that their provisions were gone, and were again forced to halt. Their camp was built on the side of the mountain, and their rifles easily supplied their wants. The journey was rigorously renewed, and after many days of further struggling, they at length found themselves on one of the tops of the [Pg 34] Allegany ridge. Here they were, upon Cumberland mountain. At this place they halted once more, to look down upon the magnificent prospect which was spread out before them. This was their first view of the new region, and they felt that it was all that Finley had described it to be. It was indeed a glorious country. The land was covered with trees and flowers; there were the rolling hills, and the beautiful valleys, and the clear sparkling streams, of which he had spoken.

The prospect was too beautiful to allow them to tarry long: they panted to be in that country. With more earnest desires than ever, they commenced descending the mountains. This part of the journey was comparatively easy. In a few days now they reached the western base of the hills, and entered a lovely plain. Here, for the first time, the new hunters saw the finest of western game—a herd of buffaloes. From the skirt of the wood at the end of the plain, a countless troop of these animals came rushing over it. The men were delighted; they had heard of these noble beasts of the forest, but none of them, except Finley, had ever seen one. As the mass came tramping toward them, they stood gazing in astonishment. Finley, who knew that men were sometimes trampled to death by these moving troops, kept his eye steadily upon the herd until the foremost was within rifle-shot; he then levelled [Pg 35] his gun, and the leader fell dead. With a wild bellow the herd parted on each side of the fallen animal, and went scampering through the plain. There seemed no end to the number, as they still came rushing from the wood. The mass appeared closing again in a solid body, when he seized Holden's rifle, and shot another. Now they were completely routed; branching off on the two sides of the plain, they went bellowing and tearing past them. "An amazing country, this!" cried Boone; "who ever beheld such an abundance?" The camp was once more soon built, a blazing fire made, and, for the first time in their lives, five of these men sat down to a supper of buffalo-meat. They talked of their new country, the quantity of game, and how joyously they would roam through the huge forests, until the night had worn far away.

The next morning, after breakfast, they packed up such portions of the animals as they could readily carry, and resumed their march. In a little time they reached Red river. Here Finley began to feel more at home, for on this river he had lived. Following the course of the stream, ere long they came to the place which had been his trading-post with the Indians. They had been more than a month reaching this point, and, naturally enough, were wearied. Finley, too, could no longer guide them; and here, for the present, they determined [Pg 36] to halt again. It was now the seventh day of June.

As this was to be their headquarters for some time, they built at once a substantial log cabin. They were now fairly in the wilds of Kentucky; and remembering that the whole region was the fighting-ground of the wandering Indians, the cabin was built not only to protect them from the weather, but to answer as a sort of fort against the savages. This shelter being provided, their whole time now was given to hunting and exploring the country. Hunting was a pastime indeed, the game was so abundant. They could look out upon herds of buffaloes scattered through the canebrakes, browsing upon the leaves of the cane, or cropping the tall grass; the deer bounded fearlessly by the very door of their hut, and wild turkeys were to be found everywhere. Everything was in a state of nature; the animals had not yet learned to be afraid of man. Of course, they did not suffer with hunger: provisions of the finest kind were ever in their cabin. But the buffaloes provided them with more than food. From time to time, as they needed moccasins for their feet, his skin supplied them; and when at night they felt the dampness of the weather, his hide was the blanket in which they wrapped themselves and slept soundly.

The country, as they wandered through it, struck them as beautiful indeed. There were the lofty [Pg 37] trees of the forest, with no undergrowth except the cane, the grass, and the flowers. They seemed to have been planted by the hand of man at regular distances. Clear streams were seen winding through lovely meadows, surrounded by the gently-sloping hills; and the fearless buffalo and deer were their companions every hour. In their wanderings they came several times to hard and well-tramped roads. It was by following these that they discovered many of the salt springs or licks where salt is made even now. The roads to these were worn thus hard by the buffaloes and other animals that were in the habit of visiting the springs.

The place of Finley's old trading-post, where their cabin now stood, seems to have been chosen by him not only as a central point for trade: it was on the side of a finely-sloping hill, and commanded a good view of the country below. The situation was beautiful. Perhaps he chose it when he was a lonely white man in the wilderness, because thence he might readily see the approach of Indians, and make his escape, or perhaps it was the very beauty of the spot that charmed him. He had a love for the beautiful. One day, he and Boone were standing by the door of the cabin. The wind was sighing in the tops of the forest, and while they were listening to the music, they were looking out upon the beautiful region below; the [Pg 38] grass was green, and the bright flowers turned up their leaves to the sun. "Glorious country!" cried Finley; "this wilderness does indeed blossom like the rose."—"Yes," replied Boone, "and who would live amid the barren pine-hills of North Carolina, to hear the screaming of the jay, and now and then shoot a deer too lean to be eaten? This is the land for hunters. Here man and beast may grow to their full size."

In this way, for more than six months, these men fearlessly hunted and roamed through the woods. Contrary to their expectations, through the whole summer they saw no Indians, nor did they meet with any remarkable adventure. The precaution of a nightly watch was adopted, but they met with no disturbance from man or beast. They had glorious sport by day, and slept quietly at night. After this, as you will see, they began to meet difficulties.

On the 22d of December, Boone and Stewart started off, as they had often done before, upon an exploring tour. After wandering several miles, they pressed their way through a piece of thick woods, and came out upon a boundless open forest. Here they found quantities of persimmon-trees, loaded with ripe fruit, while clusters of wild grapes covered the vines that were hanging from the lofty branches. Flowers were still in bloom, and scented the air; herds of animals might be seen through [Pg 39] the forest in every direction: add to this that the day was beautiful, and you will not be surprised to learn that they continued to wander—indeed, that they wandered much further than they supposed. It was nearly dark when they reached the Kentucky river, and stood looking upon its rippling waters. Perceiving a hill close by, they climbed it, that they might take a better view of the course of the stream. They were now descending, on their way homeward, when suddenly they heard an

Indian yell, and out rushed from the canebrake a party of savages. They had no time for resistance—indeed, time was nothing; they were overpowered by numbers. The savages seized them, took away their rifles and ammunition, bound them, and marched them off to their camp. The next morning they started off with their prisoners, the poor fellows not knowing where they were going, or what was to be done to them. They did not know one word of their language, and could therefore learn nothing: this much, however, they very well understood—that it would not do to show any signs of fear to the Indians; and therefore they went on cheerfully. In a little time they became better acquainted with their captors, and judged, from certain signs, that the Indians themselves had not determined what was to be done. Part seemed to be for sparing them, part for killing; still their cheer [Pg 40] fulness was the same. This apparent fearlessness deceived the Indians; they supposed the prisoners were well pleased with their condition, and did not watch them closely. On the seventh night of their march, the savages, as usual, made their camp, and all laid down to sleep. About midnight, Boone touched Stewart, and waked him: now or never was their time. They rose, groped their way to the rifles, and stole from the camp. They hardly dared to look behind them; every sound startled them, even the snapping of the twigs under their feet. Fortunately, it was dark, even if the Indians pursued. They wandered all that night and the whole of the next day, when at last, without meeting a man, they reached their own camp. But what was their surprise on finding the camp plundered, and not one of their companions to be seen? What had become of them? Perhaps they were prisoners; possibly they were murdered; or it might be that they had started back for North Carolina. They were safe, but where were their comrades? Wearied in body, and tormented with fears for their friends, they commenced preparing for the night. A sound was now heard. They seized their rifles, and stood ready, expecting the Indians. Two men were seen indistinctly approaching. "Who comes there?" cried Boone. "White men and friends," was the answer. Boone knew the voice. In an instant more, his brother [Pg 41] Squire Boone, with another man, entered the cabin. These two men had set out from Carolina for the purpose of reaching them, and had for days been wandering in search of their camp. It was a joyous meeting—the more joyous, because unexpected. Big tears were again in Daniel Boone's eyes when he heard, from his brother, that his wife and children were well. [Pg 42]

CHAPTER III.

WHEN Squire Boone had told his brother all the news of home, it became his turn to be a listener, while Daniel talked to him of all that happened since they parted. After telling him of the beautiful country, and their happy freedom as they wandered through it for six months, then came the story of his captivity and escape. That escape was but just now made, and with a full heart he dwelt upon this part of his story. It would not have been strange if Squire had now felt alarmed; but his disposition was much like his brother's: he loved the woods, and was afraid of nothing.

In a little time, the four were once more hunting freely through the forests. Signs of Indians were to be seen around, however; possibly they were [Pg 43] the very Indians who had captured them. In their wanderings, therefore, they kept together usually, for self-protection. One day, they started out upon a buffalo-hunt. As they came upon a herd of these animals, Stewart lodged his ball in one of them, without bringing him down. The buffalo went tearing through the forest; and Daniel Boone, with Stewart, forgetful of everything else, went chasing after him. Naturally enough, like excited men, they had no idea how far they had travelled, until their very weariness reminded them that it was time to turn back. Tired as he was, a harder race was now before Boone. They had scarcely started on their return, when a party of Indians rushed from the canebrake, and let fly their arrows. Stewart fell dead on the spot. Boone would have fired his rifle, but he felt it was useless: he could kill but one man; his only chance of escape was in flight. With Indian yells and arrows close behind him, he leaped forward, and, by tremendous exertions, at last distanced his pursuers. When he reached the camp, he fell, completely exhausted.

The party, now cut down to three, was in a little time reduced to two. From some cause or other, they could not tell what—possibly the sad story of Stewart's death, and the fear of like troubles—the companion who had come out with Squire Boone determined upon returning to North [Pg 44] Carolina. Very soon, therefore, he left them alone in the wilderness. [2]

It is not strange that, being thus deserted, Squire Boone felt restless and dissatisfied; the wonder is, that Daniel was not dissatisfied likewise. But he was happy and contented, and often struggled to call up the same feelings in his brother. "You see," he would often say, "how little nature requires, to be satisfied. Happiness, the companion of content, is rather found in our own breasts than in the enjoyment of external things. I firmly believe it requires but a little philosophy to make a man happy in whatsoever state he is. This consists in a full resignation to the will of Providence; and a resigned soul finds pleasure in a path strewed with briars and thorns." This was good counsel, my young friends, and I hope you will bear it with you through life. It will serve to comfort you as much as it did Squire Boone.

To be idle, was to allow time for this melancholy, and Daniel Boone kept his brother constantly busy. The Indians, they were certain, [Pg 45] knew where their present camp was, and therefore they resolved to make another. After choosing their spot, they employed themselves industriously in erecting another cabin, which might serve to shelter them through the coming winter. This being finished, they went to their old sport, wandering through the woods, admiring the country, and bringing down now and then a buffalo or a deer with their rifles. At night, they would return to their camp, raise a fire, cook their supper, and sit till long after midnight, talking of their old home on the Yadkin. Squire forgot his loneliness, and became quite satisfied. In this way time rolled off until the winter had passed away, and spring appeared. Strangely enough, they had been undisturbed; they had met not even with one Indian.

They had learned in the wilderness to dispense well nigh with all comforts; food and sleep were all they expected. But their powder and shot were now beginning to run low, and without these they could not long procure food. It was necessary, therefore, to make some arrangement whereby they might obtain a fresh supply. Their plan was soon settled: Squire Boone was to go back to North Carolina, and return with ammunition. They supposed horses would be valuable, also, and he was likewise to bring with him two of these. Perilous as the plan was, Squire agreed to bear his part in it, and Daniel as cheerfully consented to his. Accordingly, [Pg 46] on the first day of May, Squire set off for the Yadkin; and, as if nothing was to be wanting to leave Daniel in perfect loneliness, their only dog followed Squire as he started.

Here, then, Daniel Boone was left entirely alone. Here he was a sort of Robinson Crusoe in the wilderness—with this difference, that Robinson was shipwrecked, and had no choice; while Boone chose the wilderness as his home. He was now completely the "man of the woods"—far away, hundreds of miles from any white settlement. For the first time in his life, according to his own confession, he felt lonely. His mind was filled with the remembrance of his wife and children, and the thought that he should never see them again. He knew, however, that sad thoughts, when indulged in, will grow very rapidly, and therefore dismissed them.

For safety's sake now, he changed his camp every night, that he might avoid the Indians. Sometimes he slept in the canebrake; sometimes he laid himself by the side of a stream; sometimes in the caves of the rocks. By day he was surrounded by his old companions the buffaloes and deer, and at night was not unfrequently disturbed by the howling of the wolves. He roamed over many a beautiful tract of country. Now he would ascend a hill, and look down upon the scene spread like a map before him; now he would trace some stream [Pg 47] to its source, or, following the well-tramped roads of the buffaloes, would find some spring bubbling in the forest. In this way he moved over a large part of the country. At one time, he struck the Ohio river, and wandered for days on the banks of that noble stream. It is said, that in his rambles, he one day stood upon the spot where the city of Louisville now stands. He learned to love the woods more than ever. Long after this, he used to declare, that "no crowded city, with all its commerce and noble buildings, could give him as much pleasure as the beauty of Kentucky at that time afforded him."

Fortunately, he met no Indians. At one time he came in sight of a roving party, but managed to escape from them. The mode in which he escaped will show you his perfect self-possession. He had stopped one day to rest under the shade of a tree, when suddenly he spied the party in the distance. This was enough for him. He immediately commenced his course through the forest, hoping that they had not seen him, and therefore would not pursue. From time to time he would look back through the woods; and at length became convinced, to his sorrow, that if they had not seen him, they had marked his tracks, and were now on his trail. He pushed on for more than two miles, trying in various ways to break the trail, and thus put them out; still, as he looked [Pg 48] back, he could see that they were following him He was puzzled to know what to do. A happy thought now struck him. He had just passed the brow of a small hill; the heavy grape-vines were hanging from the trees all around him. He seized one of these, and, bracing himself against the tree with his feet, threw himself as far as he could. This broke the trail, and he now kept directly on from the spot where he landed, in a different direction. The Indians came up, tracking him as far as the tree: were then lost, and gave up the chase.

Another adventure is told of him during his lonely wanderings, more perilous even than this. One day he heard a strange noise in the woods; he could see nothing, but stood ready with his rifle. Presently an immense she-bear was seen approaching him. Surrounded by her young cubs, she was doubly fierce. As she came near, Boone levelled his rifle and fired. Unfortunately, his steady eye failed this time; the ball did not strike as he had aimed, and the animal pressed forward, the more enraged. It was impossible to load again: the bear was upon him; he had only time to draw his hunting-knife from his belt. The bear laid her paws on him, and drew him toward her. The rifle in his left hand was a sort of guard, while with his right he pointed the knife directly for the heart of the animal. As she grasped him, the knife entered her body, and she fell dead. [Pg 49]

As the time drew near for the return (as he thought) of his brother, Boone went back to the old camp where they had lodged together, to meet him. Here day after day he kept his lookout—day after day he was disappointed. He began now to be very sad. He did not doubt his brother's fidelity; he knew he would not desert him; but there were many dangers by the way, and perhaps he had perished. Then he thought, too, of his wife and little ones. If that brother had perished, he likewise must die without seeing them. Without ammunition to procure food, or defend himself, what could he do? He must die, there in the wilderness. His brother had been absent now nearly three months: surely it was time for his return. Another day of disappointment was now drawing to a close, as Boone sat, sick at heart, by the door of his cabin. A sound broke on his ear; he rose and stood listening, with his hand on the lock of his rifle. It was the tread of horses. The next moment he saw his brother through the forest leading two horses heavily laden. Here was abundance of ammunition and other comfort. The evening of the 27th of July was long after this remembered by Daniel Boone as one of the most joyous of his life.

A fire was soon made, their supper cooked, and long after midnight they sat talking. Thousands of questions were asked and answered, until, [Pg 50] wearied out, at last they lay down to sleep. The sun was high in the heavens when they waked in the morning.

After breakfast, Daniel Boone proposed a new plan to his brother. Much as he loved the woods, he felt that two men could hardly be safe in the neighborhood of so many Indians. Moreover he longed to see his family: the stories of Squire had called up fresh recollections in his heart. The plan therefore was, to select a suitable spot for their home, then return to Carolina and bring out his family. Squire readily assented to this; and now they employed themselves for several days in hunting and laying in a supply of provisions. This being done, they went to the Cumberland river, and wandered for some time along the stream without finding a place to please them. Roaming about now, they found many new streams, to which, as the first discoverers, they gave names. Anxious as they were to return to the Yadkin, they were in no such hurry as to neglect making a full survey. The whole winter passed away before they pleased themselves. At length they came upon the Kentucky river. Here the lands delighted them. On the banks of this stream they determined to make their settlement, and now (March, 1771) turned their faces homeward. As he left the chosen spot, Boone says that "he felt it was a second paradise, and was resolved, at the [Pg 51] risk of his life and fortune, that his family should have a home there."

As they journeyed eastward from the Kentucky river, they occasionally blazed their pathway (as huntsmen say) that they might find their way back. It was necessary thus to leave some track through the forest wilderness, that they might again reach their chosen spot. [3] Fortunately they met with no Indians.

We hear of but one adventure on their way homeward. After travelling quietly several days, they were one morning startled by a noise. Presently a herd of buffaloes came rushing and tearing through the forest; they seemed frantic. The cause of all this was soon seen. A panther, seated upon the back of one of the buffaloes, had plunged his claws and teeth into him. The blood was streaming down his sides, and the poor animal, struggling to shake him off, rushed into the midst of the herd. This frightened the rest, and they went bellowing and dashing through the woods. Daniel Boone raised his rifle, and sent a ball through the panther. He fell dead. Not far off they met a pack of wolves, following as usual in [Pg 52] the track of the buffaloes. For the fun of seeing them scatter, Squire now fired his rifle, and away they went, scampering in all directions.

In due time they came to the mountains. After trying to ascend in various places, at length they found a narrow and rugged gap, through which with great difficulty they made their way. It was, however, the best pass they could discover, and they blazed their track, that they might find it again. In a little time now, Daniel Boone was again in his cabin on the banks of the Yadkin. I need hardly say there was a joyous meeting; he was once more happy in the bosom of his family. He had been absent nearly two years.

Amid the joys of home, however, he did not forget his chosen spot in Kentucky; his heart was filled with the thought that his happy home might be happier there. As this was to be his final move, it was necessary to settle all his business on the Yadkin; and as he had tried the wilderness, he felt that a few trusty companions would be invaluable in that new region. He commenced, therefore, making what he thought proper preparations for a return. To beat up such neighbors as they desired, he and Squire gave glowing accounts of the new country; the rich lands, the forests, the streams, the flowers, and the game, were all talked of. They saw only, and consequently spoke only, of the bright side of the picture. [Pg 53] But there were numbers of people to talk of difficulties; these spoke of the folly of the Boones, in thinking of making such a country their home, and the madness of any man who should think of following them; the country was wild, and all who settled there must suffer many privations: then, too (according to their story), it was afflicted with terrible diseases, and they might all expect to die there, or, if they escaped the climate, they must fall into the hands of the fierce and cruel Indians who roamed through those forests; the place they declared was so dangerous that it was known, wherever it was known, as "the dark and bloody ground." With these sad stories floating about continually, it is not wonderful that the Boones found difficulty in beating up companions, and that more than two years passed away before they were ready for a start. At the end of that time they found that, while many were opposed to them, and others wavering as to what they would do, there were some, prompted by a spirit of bold adventure, ready to join them. Five families were willing to go with them to Kentucky.

Daniel Boone now sold his farm, and all things being made ready, on the 25th of September, 1773, the little company bade farewell to their friends and started for the west, driving before them their flocks and their herds. In their route, not a great [Pg 54] way from the Yadkin, was the settlement of Powel's valley. The story of their plan had spread through the neighborhood, and when they reached this spot they were delighted to find that the people were not so timid as those on the Yadkin: forty men here joined the party. Now they travelled on in high spirits; the whole body, old and young, numbering between seventy and eighty souls.

In a little time they came to the mountains, and found the pathway blazed by the Boones. In less than a fortnight they passed the first ridge of the Alleganies, known as "Powel's range," and were now quietly descending the second, known as "Walden's range," when sorrow overtook them. They were in a dark and narrow gap, when the wild yell of Indians broke upon their ears. The savages rushed into the gap behind them, and let fly their arrows. Six of the party fell dead, a seventh was wounded. The men rallied around the women and children; the first discharge of their rifles scattered the savages. But the mischief was done; the sudden attack of the Indians was like a flash of lightning; they were seen only for an instant; yet, like the lightning, they had done their work: there were the dead, and alas! among them was the oldest son of Daniel Boone.

The party, a little time before so happy, was [Pg 55] now in deep sorrow. What was to be done? The Indians had not only killed their companions, but their flocks and herds had all fled in fright, and could not be again gathered together. In dismay, the greater part were for retreating instantly to the nearest white settlement; this was upon the Clinch river, forty miles behind them. The Boones begged them to keep on their way—not to think of turning back; but it was all to no purpose; most of them insisted on retreating, and they at length yielded to the general desire. Accordingly, the dead were decently buried, and in great sadness they all traced their way back to Clinch river.

Here Daniel Boone remained with his family eight months. At the end of that time he was requested by Governor Dunmore, of Virginia, to go to the falls of the Ohio, to serve as a guide to a party of surveyors who had been sent there some months before. The western country was now beginning to attract attention, and the Indians were becoming very hostile to the whites. Accordingly, on the 6th of June, 1774, he started (with one man, Michael Stoner), and without any accident reached the point at which he aimed—the spot where Louisville now stands. The service for the surveyors was promptly performed, and they were enabled to complete their work, while Boone was at liberty to return to his family. [Pg 56] It is remarkable that he made this journey on foot, a distance of eight hundred miles, through a trackless wilderness, in the short period of sixty-two days.

He was not allowed to remain quiet long; soon after his return, the Indians northwest of the Ohio, especially the Shawanese, made open war upon the whites. Governor Dunmore felt bound to protect his countrymen, and, among other acts for their defence, sent Daniel Boone, with the title of captain, to take command of three garrisons. This service was likewise well performed; matters were soon more quiet, the soldiers were discharged, and Boone was relieved from his post.

He had not been a wanderer in the woods in vain; his fame had gone abroad, and his services were in the following spring sought again. A company of gentlemen in North Carolina—the principal man of whom was Colonel Richard Henderson—were attempting to purchase the lands on the south side of the Kentucky river, from the Cherokee Indians. [4] They had agreed to hold a treaty with the Indians, at Wataga, in March, 1775, to settle the boundaries of their intended purchase, and they now desired Boone to attend that treaty, and manage their business. In compliance with their wish, he went to Wataga, and [Pg 57] performed their service so well, that they gave him further employment. He was now requested to mark out a road from their settlement, through the wilderness, to Kentucky river. This was a work of great labor. It was necessary to make many surveys to find the best route, and when the best was found, it was, much of it, over mountains and rugged regions. With a number of laborers, he commenced the work. He met with two attacks from the Indians by the way, in which four of his men were killed, and five wounded. Undaunted, he pushed resolutely on, and, in the month of April, reached the Kentucky river. To guard themselves from the savages, they immediately commenced the building of a fort at a salt lick, about sixty yards from the south bank of the stream. The Indians annoyed them from time to time, while they were thus engaged, but fortunately killed but one man. On the 14th day of June the fort was finished, and Boone started back for his family on Clinch river. As an honor to him, the party gave to this first settlement in the wilderness of Kentucky the name of Boonesborough.

He reached his family without accident, and, as rapidly as he could, retraced his way with them through the forest. The fort consisted of several cabins, surrounded by pickets ten feet high, planted firmly in the ground. In one of these, Daniel [Pg 58] Boone found a shelter for his family. The long desire of his heart was at last gratified: he had a home in Kentucky. He was the first settler of that region, and (as he proudly said) his "wife and daughter the first white women that ever stood on the banks of Kentucky river." [Pg 59]

CHAPTER IV.

IT was now the season of autumn; the trees had not yet shed their leaves, and the forests were still beautiful. Mrs. Boone felt happy as she looked upon her new home. Winter came, and glided rapidly and joyously away. With their axes and rifles, the men in the settlement brought in constant and ample supplies of fuel and game, and around the blazing hearth of Daniel Boone there was not one in the family who sighed for the old home on the Yadkin. Boone naturally supposed that a fear of the Indians would be the principal trouble with his wife; and well she might dread them, remembering the loss of her son formerly in the pass of the mountains. Fortunately, however, she did not see an Indian through the season. But one white man was killed by them during the winter, and he lost his life by unfortunately wandering away from [Pg 60] the fort unarmed. After this, the other settlers were more prudent; they never went without the pickets for fuel without taking their rifles.

When spring opened, they were soon very busy. A small clearing without the pickets was first made for a garden-spot. Mrs. Boone and her daughter brought out their stock of garden-seeds, and commenced cultivating this, while the men went on earnestly in the work of preparing for their fields. They were calculating that they were making their homes for life. Day after day the neighborhood resounded with the crash of falling trees, as these hardy men levelled the forests. While they were thus engaged, they were made happy by a new arrival. Colonel Calloway, an old companion of Boone's, led by the desire of finding his old friend and a new country, came out to the settlement this spring, and brought with him his two young daughters. Here, then, were companions for Boone's daughter. The fathers were happy, and the mother and girls delighted.

Spring had not passed away, however, before they were in sorrow about these children. When the wild flowers began to bloom in the woods, the girls were in the habit of strolling around the fort and gathering them to adorn their humble homes. This was an innocent and pleasant occupation; it pleased the girls as well as their parents. [Pg 61] They were only cautioned not to wander far, for fear of the Indians. This caution, it seems, was forgotten. Near the close of a beautiful day in July, they were wandering, as usual, and the bright flowers tempted them to stroll thoughtlessly onward. Indians were in ambush; they were suddenly surrounded, seized, and hurried away, in spite of their screams for help. They were carried by their captors to the main body of the Indian party, some miles distant. Night came, and the girls did not return; search was made for them, and they were nowhere to be found. The thought now flashed upon Boone that the children were prisoners; the Indians had captured them. The parents were well nigh frantic: possibly the girls were murdered. Boone declared that he would recover his child, if alive, if he lost his own life in the effort. The whole settlement was at once roused: every man offered to start off with the two fathers in search of the children. But Boone would not have them all; some must remain behind, to protect the settlement. Of the whole number he chose seven; he and Calloway headed them; and, in less time than I have been telling the story, laden with their knapsacks and rifles, they were off in pursuit.

Which way were they to go? It was a long time before they could find a track of the party. The wily Indians, as usual, had used all their cunning [Pg 62] in hiding their footprints and breaking their trail. Covering their tracks with leaves; walking at right angles occasionally from the main path; crossing brooks by walking in them for some time, and leaving them at a point far from where they entered: all this had been practised, and I presume that the fathers never would have got on the track if the girls had not been as cunning as their captors. After wandering about for some time, they came at length to a brook, and waded along it for a great while in search of footprints. They looked faithfully far up and down the stream, for they knew the Indian stratagem. Presently Calloway leaped up for joy. "God bless my child!" cried he; "they have gone this way." He had picked up a little piece of riband which one of his daughters had dropped, purposely to mark the trail. Now they were on the track. Travelling on as rapidly as they could, from time to time they picked up shreds of handkerchiefs, or fragments of their dresses, that the girls had scattered by the way. Before the next day ended, they were still more clearly on the track. They reached a soft, muddy piece of ground, and found all the footprints of the party; they were now able to tell the number of the Indians. The close of the next day brought them still nearer to the objects of their search. Night had set in; they were still wandering on, when, upon reaching a small hill, [Pg 63] they saw a camp-fire in the distance. They were now delighted; this surely was the party that had captured the girls. Everything was left to the management of Boone. He brought his men as near the fire as he dared approach, and sheltered them from observation under the brow of a hill. Calloway and another man were then selected from the group; the rest were told that they might go to sleep: they were, however, to sleep on their arms, ready to start instantly at a given signal. Calloway was to go with Boone; the other man was stationed on the top of the hill, to give the alarm, if necessary. The two parents now crept cautiously onward to a covert of bushes not far from the fire. Looking through, they saw fifteen or twenty Indians fast asleep in the camp; but where were the girls? Crawling to another spot, they pushed the bushes cautiously aside, and, to their great joy, saw in another camp the daughters sleeping in each other's arms. Two Indians with their tomahawks guarded this camp. One seemed to be asleep. They crept gently around in the rear of this. They were afraid to use their rifles: the report would wake the other camp. Calloway was to stand ready to shoot the sleeping Indian if he stirred, while Boone was to creep behind the other, seize, and strangle him. They were then to hurry off with the children. Unfortunately, they calculated wrong: the [Pg 64] Indianwhom they supposed to be sleeping was wide awake, and, as Boone drew near, his shadow was seen by this man. He sprang up, and the woods rang with his yell. The other camp was roused; the Indians came rushing to this. Boone's first impulse was to use his rifle, but Calloway's prudence restrained him. Had he fired, it would have been certain destruction to parents and children. They surrendered themselves prisoners, pleading earnestly at the same time for their captive daughters. The Indians bound them with cords, placed guards over them, and then retired to their camp. The poor girls, roused by the tumult, now saw their parents in this pitiable condition. Here they were, likewise made captives, for their love of them.

There was no more sleep in the Indian camp that night. Till the dawn of the day they were talking of what should be done to the new prisoners: some were for burning them at the stake; others objected to this. Boone and Calloway were to be killed, but they were too brave to be killed in this way. Some proposed making them run the gauntlet. At last it was decided (in pity for the girls, it is said) that the parents should be killed in a more decent and quiet way. They were to be tomahawked and scalped, and the girls were still to be kept prisoners. With the morning's light they started out to execute the sentence. That the poor girls might not see their parents murdered [Pg 65] the men were led off to the woods, and there lashed to two trees. Two of the savages stood before them with their tomahawks, while the rest were singing and dancing around them. At length the tomahawks were lifted to strike them; at that instant the crack of rifles was heard, and the two Indians fell dead. Another and another report was heard: others fell, and the rest fled in dismay. Boone's companions had saved them. All night long they had waited for the signal: none had been given; they had heard the Indian yell; they feared that they were taken. They had watched the camp with the greatest anxiety, and now had delivered them. They were instantly untied; the girls were quickly released, and in the arms of their parents; and they all started joyously homeward. Mrs. Boone was delighted to see them. The party had been so long gone, that she feared her husband and child were alike lost to her for ever.

It is not surprising that when men found out that a settlement had been made in Kentucky, others were soon ready to start off for that fertile region. Accordingly, we find many arriving this year, and settling themselves in the country. Harrod, Logan, Ray, Wagin, Bowman, and many other fearless spirits, now threw themselves, like Boone, into the heart of the wilderness, and made their forts, or stations, as they were called. These were just like the home of Boone—nothing [Pg 66] more than a few log cabins, surrounded by pickets. Indeed, the country began now to assume so much importance in the eyes of men, that the Governor of Virginia thought proper to take some notice of it. When the legislature met, he recommended that the southwestern part of the county of Fincastle—which meant all the large tract of country west of the Alleganies now known as Kentucky—should be made into a separate county, by the name of Kentucky. The legislature thought it well to follow his advice. The new county was made, and had the privilege of sending two members to the Virginia legislature.

Nor is it surprising that the Indians began now to be more violent than ever in their enmity. They had been unwilling before that a white man should cross their path as they roamed over their hunting-grounds; but now, when they saw clearings made, and houses built, they felt that the whites meant to drive them for ever from that region. Their hatred consequently increased now every hour. Another circumstance at this time served to rouse them the more against the settlers. If you will think of the period of which I am speaking (the year 1776), perhaps you may guess what it was. The colonists of America in that year, you will remember, declared themselves independent of Great Britain. In the war which followed (known among us always as the [Pg 67] Revolutionary War), England struggled hard to subdue them; nor was she always choice as to the means which she used for the purpose. She did not hesitate even to rouse the red men of the forests, and give them arms to fight the colonists. They were not only turned loose upon them with their own tomahawks and scalping-knives, but were well supplied with British rifles and balls. All the new settlements in the land were troubled with them, and Kentucky had to bear her part of the sorrow. These Indians would scatter themselves in small parties, and hang secretly for days and nights around the infant stations. Until one is acquainted with Indian stratagems, he can hardly tell how cunning these people are. By day they would hide themselves in the grass, or behind the stumps of trees, near the pathways to the fields or springs of water, and it was certain death to the white man who travelled that way. At night they would creep up to the very gateway of the pickets, and watch for hours for a white man. If any part of his person was exposed, he was sure to catch a rifle-ball. It was impossible to discover them, even when their mischief was done. They would lie in the grass flat on their bellies for days, almost under the very palisades. Sometimes an Indian yell would be heard near one point of the fort, startling all the settlers—a yell raised only to [Pg 68] draw them all in one direction, while the Indians did their mischief in another. In this sneaking mode of warfare, men, women, and children, were killed in many places; and not unfrequently whole droves of cattle were cut off.

At length, to the great joy of the settlers, the Indians began to show themselves more boldly: for anything was better than these secret ambushes of the savages; an open enemy is not so much to be dreaded as a secret one. Boonesborough and Harrodsburgh (a settlement made by James Harrod, a bold adventurer from the banks of the Monongahela) were now the principal stations. Toward these, new emigrants were from time to time moving, and against these stations, as being the strongest, the Indians felt the greatest hatred, and directed their principal attacks. Early in the spring of 1777, a party was moving toward Harrodsburgh: fortunately, the Indians attacked them; for, though two whites were killed, the attack probably saved the settlement. It was only four miles from the place, and the Indians were now on their way there. One young man escaped in the midst of the fight to give the alarm at Harrodsburgh. The station was instantly put in a state of defence. Ere long, the Indians appeared. A brisk firing at once commenced on both sides; the savages saw one of their men fall, and finding that they were not likely to gain any advantage, [Pg 69] soon scattered for the woods. The whites lost one man also, and three were slightly wounded.

On the 15th of April, a party of one hundred savages appeared boldly before Boonesborough. Every man of them was armed with his gun, as well as bow and arrows. Boone, however, was prepared for them, and gave them a warm reception—so warm, that they soon gladly retreated. How many of their men were killed it was impossible to tell, for they dragged away their dead with them. In the fort one man was killed, and four were badly wounded.

Their loss this time only served to make them more revengeful. In July following they again came against Boonesborough, resolved upon vengeance. They numbered this time more than two hundred. To prevent any of the white settlements from sending aid to Boonesborough, they had sent off small parties to molest them, and keep them busy. The savages now commenced their attack, and for two days a constant firing was kept up. At last, finding their efforts again idle, they raised a loud yell, and returned to the forests. The whites could now count their slain and wounded as they dragged them off: seven were killed, and numbers wounded, while in the fort only one white man was slain. In spite of their numbers and their cunning, they did but little harm: for Boone was never found sleeping; he knew that Indians [Pg 70] were his neighbors, and he was always ready for them. After this, they learned to dread him more than ever. He now went by the name of the "*Great Long Knife*."

Attacks of this kind were made from time to time openly against the settlements, but especially against these two principal stations. They all ended very much in the same way, and it would only weary you if I should attempt to speak of them. It is enough for you to know that the whites were always on the lookout, and that Boone was regarded as their principal leader and protector. We will pass on, therefore, to something more interesting.

I have already stated that the stations of these settlers were usually built, for comfort's sake, in the neighborhood of salt licks or springs; and near such a lick, as you will remember, Boonesborough stood. The supply of salt, however, was not sufficient; new settlers were often arriving, and it became necessary to seek a place which would afford more of that article. Boone was the father of the settlement, and he undertook to find it. Having selected thirty men as his companions, on the 1st of January, 1778, he started for the Blue Licks, on Licking river—a stream, as you know, emptying itself into the Ohio opposite where Cincinnati now stands. Upon reaching this spot, the thirty men were soon very busy in making salt. [Pg 71] Boone, having no taste for the work, sauntered off to employ himself in shooting game for the company. He had wandered some distance from the river one day, when suddenly he came upon two Indians armed with muskets. It was impossible for him to retreat, and the chances were against him if he stood. His usual coolness did not forsake him; he instantly jumped behind a tree. As the Indians came within gun-shot, he exposed himself on the side of the tree: one savage immediately fired, and Boone dodged the ball. One shot was thus thrown away, and this was just what he desired. Exposing himself immediately in precisely the same way, the other musket was discharged by the other Indian, to as little purpose. He now stepped boldly out; the Indians were trying hard to load again; he raised his rifle, and one savage fell dead. He was now on equal terms with the other. Drawing his hunting-knife, he leaped forward and placed his foot upon the body of the dead Indian; the other raised his tomahawk to strike but Boone, with his rifle in his left hand, warded off the blow, while with his right he plunged his knife into the heart of the savage. His two foes lay dead before him. If you should ever visit Washington city, you will see a memorial of this deed. The act is in sculpture, over the southern door of the rotundo of the capitol.

After this he continued his hunting excursions as usual, for the [Pg 72] benefit of his party; but he was not so fortunate the next time he met with Indians. On the 7th of February, as he was roaming through the woods, he saw a party of one hundred savages on their way to attack Boonesborough. His only chance for escape now was to run. He instantly fled, but the swiftest warriors gave chase, and before a great while he was overtaken and made a prisoner. He was, of all men, the one whom they desired to take; they could now gain, as they thought, some information about Boonesborough. They now carried him back to the Blue Licks. As they drew near, Boone, knowing that it was idle to resist, made signs to the salt-makers to surrender themselves. This they did, and thus the savages soon had in their possession twenty-eight captives. Fortunately for themselves, three of the men had started homeward with a supply of salt, and thus escaped.

Now was the time for the savages to have attacked Boonesborough; for, with the loss of so many men, and Boone their leader, we may readily suppose that the station might have surrendered. Flushed, however, with the capture of their prisoners, they seem not to have thought of it any longer.

The prisoners were marched immediately to Old Chilicothe, the principal Indian town on the Little Miami, where they arrived on the [Pg 73] 18th. There was great rejoicing over them when they reached this old settlement of the savages, though Boone says they were "treated as kindly as prisoners could expect." Early in the next month Boone with ten of his men was marched off to Detroit by forty Indians. Here Governor Hamilton, the British commander of that post, treated them with much kindness. The ten men were soon delivered up for a small ransom. But when the Governor offered them one hundred pounds to give up Boone, that he might allow him to return home, they refused to part with him; they looked upon him as too dangerous an enemy to be allowed to go free upon any terms. Several English gentlemen were moved with pity when they saw Boone thus a helpless prisoner, and offered to supply his wants. He thanked them for their feeling, but refused to receive any aid, stating that he never expected to be able to return their kindness, and therefore was unwilling to receive it. The truth was, he was not disposed to receive assistance from the enemies of his country.

With no other prisoner than Boone, the party now started again for Old Chilicothe. As they drew near, after a very fatiguing march, Boone thought he understood why they had refused to part with him. Before they entered the village, they shaved his head, painted his face, and dressed him like themselves; they then placed in his [Pg 74] hands a long white staff, ornamented with deers' tails. The chief of the party then raised a yell, and all the warriors from the village answered it, and soon made their appearance. Four young warriors commenced singing as they came toward him. The two first, each bearing a calumet, took him by the arms and marched him to a cabin in the village; here he was to remain until his fate was made known to him. Of all strange customs of the Indians (and he had seen many of them), this was the strangest to him. It is not wonderful that he thought he was now to die.

Yet this was a common custom (it is said) among the Shawanese, who inhabited this village. Prisoners were often thus carried to some cabin, and then the Indian living in the cabin decided what should be done—whether the prisoner should die, or be adopted into the tribe. It happened that in this cabin lived an old Indian woman, who had lately lost a son in battle. She, of course, was to decide Boone's fate. She looked at him earnestly, admired his noble bearing and cheerful face, and at length declared that he should live. He should be her son, she said; he should be to her the son whom she had lost. The young warriors instantly announced to him his fate, and the fact was soon proclaimed through the village. Food was brought out and set before him; and every effort, which Indian love could think of, was used to make him happy. He was fairly one of the tribe; and the old [Pg 75] woman who was to be his mother was especially delighted.

He was now as free as the rest; his only sorrow was that he had to live among them. He knew, too, that if he should be caught trying to make his escape, it would be certain death to him. He pretended, therefore, to be cheerful and happy; and fortunately his old habits enabled him to play his part well. Like them, he was a man of the woods, and as fond of hunting as any of them. They all soon became attached to him, and treated him with the utmost confidence.

Sometimes large parties would go out to try their skill at their sports of racing and shooting at a mark. Boone was always with them; he knew, however, that in trials of this kind the Indians were always jealous if they were beaten, and therefore he had to act very prudently. At racing, they could excel him; but at shooting, he was more than a match for any of them. Still, when the target was set up, he was always certain to be beaten. If he shot too well, they would be jealous and angry; if he shot badly, they would hold him in contempt: and therefore he would manage to make good shots, and yet never be the successful man. He knew too much of Indians not to conduct himself properly.

Sometimes they would start out upon hunting parties. Here Boone was [Pg 76] at home; there was no jealousy when he brought down a buffalo or a deer with his rifle-ball. He might do his best; they were true hunters themselves, and were delighted with every successful shot. Returning to the village, Boone would always visit the Shawanese chief, and present him a portion of his game. By this kindness and civility he completely won the heart of the chief, and was not unfrequently consulted by him on important matters. Thus he passed his time, joining in all their modes of living; he was beloved by the old woman, the chief, and all the tribe: and none suspected that he was not contented and happy.

On the 1st of June, a large party was starting from the village for the salt-licks on the Scioto, to make salt. Boone pretended to be indifferent whether he went or not. The truth was, however, that he was very anxious to go, for he thought it would afford a fine opportunity for him to escape. He seemed so indifferent about the matter, that the party urged him to accompany them, and off he started. For ten days most of them were busy making salt, while Boone and two or three of the best marksmen hunted for the benefit of the rest. He watched his chance for escape, but none occurred; he was closely observed, it was impossible for him to attempt it. To his great sorrow, he was forced to return home with the salt-makers. [Pg 77]

They had scarcely got back, when the whole village was summoned to the council-house, to attend a council of war. Boone, as belonging to one of the principal families, went to this council. Here he met four hundred and fifty armed Indians, all gayly painted. One of the oldest warriors then struck a large drum, and marched with the war-standard three times round the council-house: this was the sure signal that they were about to make war upon some enemy. But who was the enemy? What was Boone's surprise when it was announced that they meant to attack Boonesborough! He resolved now that he would escape, even at every hazard, and alarm the settlement. Still his prudence did not forsake him.

The old warriors at once commenced gathering together a supply of parched corn, and beating up more recruits for the expedition.

All the new men (Boone among the rest, for he was forced to join them) were then marched off to the "winter-house" to drink the war-drink. This was a mixture of water and bitter herbs and roots, and was to be drank steadily for three days, during which time no man was to eat a morsel. Even if a deer or buffalo passed by, no man was to kill it; the fast must be kept. In fact, no man was allowed even to sit down, or rest himself by leaning against a tree. This was done by the old men to purify the young warriors, as they said, and to gain the [Pg 78] favor of the Great Spirit. All this was a common practice with the tribe before they went to battle; and the more strictly the fast was kept, the greater (as they supposed) were the chances of success. During these three days, Boone, like the rest, kept the fast, drank the war-drink, and did not even leave the "medicine-ground."

The fast being over, they fired their guns, yelled, danced, and sang; and in the midst of this noise the march commenced. The leading war-chief, bearing the medicine-bag, or budget (as it was called), went before; the rest followed in single file. Nothing but shouting and yelling, and the noise of guns, was heard, as they passed through the village. When they reached the woods, all the noise ceased; they were fairly on their march, and that march was to be made after the Indian fashion, in dead silence. For several days this dead march was kept up, Boone looking every hour for his chance of escape. At length, early one morning, a deer dashed by the line. Boone leaped eagerly after him, and started in pursuit. No sooner was he out of sight of the Indians, than he pressed for Boonesborough. He knew they would give chase, and therefore he doubled his track, waded in streams, and did everything that he could to throw them off his trail. Every sound startled him; he thought the Indians were behind him. With no food but roots and berries, and scarcely time to devour these, he pushed [Pg 79] through swamps and thickets for his old home. Now or never was his chance for liberty, and as such he used it. At length, after wandering nearly two hundred miles, on the fourth day he reached Boonesborough in safety. [Pg 80]

CHAPTER V.

BEFORE we go on, let me tell you of some of the curious customs which Boone noticed among the Indians, during his captivity. He had a fine opportunity for observation, and I think these strange customs will interest you.

It is not wonderful that Indian men and women are so hardy; they are trained to it from their youth: and Boone tells us how they are trained. When a child is only eight years old, this training commences; he is then made to fast frequently half a day; when he is twelve, he is made to fast a whole day. During the time of this fast, the child is left alone, and his face is always blacked. This mode of hardening them is kept up with girls until they are fourteen—with boys until they are eighteen. At length, when a [Pg 81] boy has reached the age of eighteen, his parents tell him that his education is completed, and that he is old enough to be a man! His face is now to be blacked for the last time. He is taken to a solitary cabin far away from the village; his face is blacked, and then his father makes to him a speech of this kind: "My son, the Great Spirit has allowed you to live to see this day. We have all noticed your conduct since I first began to black your face. All people will understand whether you have followed your father's advice, and they will treat you accordingly. You must now remain here until I come after you." The lad is then left alone. His father then goes off hunting, as though nothing had happened, and leaves his boy to bear his hunger as long it is possible for him to starve and live. At length he prepares a great feast, gathers his friends together, and then returns. The lad is then brought home, his face is washed in cold water, his hair is shaved, leaving nothing but the scalp-lock; they all commence eating, but the food of the lad is placed before him in a separate dish. This being over, a looking-glass and a bag of paint are then presented to him. Then they all praise him for his firmness, and tell him that he is a man. Strange as it may seem, a boy is hardly ever known to break his fast when he is blacked this way for the last time. It is looked upon as something base, and they have a [Pg 82] dread that the Great Spirit will punish them if they are disobedient to their parents.

Another curious habit which surprised Boone was that of continually changing names. A white man carries the same name from the cradle to the grave, but among these people it was very different. Their principal arms, as you know, are the tomahawk and scalping-knife, and he who can take the greatest number of scalps is the greatest man. From time to time, as warriors would return from an attack upon some enemy, these new names would begin to be known. Each man would count the number of scalps he had taken, and a certain number entitled him to a new name, in token of his bravery. It is not wonderful that they were revengeful, when they were stimulated by this sort of ambition. Besides this, they believed that he who took the scalp of a brave man received at once all his courage and other good qualities; and this made them more eager in their thirst for scalps. In this way, names of warriors were sometimes changed three or four times in a year.

Marriages in this tribe were conducted very decently. When a young warrior desired to marry, he assembled all his friends, and named the woman whom he wished for his wife. His relations then received his present, and took it to the parents of the young woman. If they were pleased with the proposal, they would dress the young woman in her [Pg 83] gayest clothes, and take her, with bundles of presents, to the friends of the warrior; then, if she pleased, she was to be married. There was no compulsion in the matter. If she was not satisfied, she had only to return his present to the young warrior, and this was considered a refusal.

Their mode of burying their dead was very much like that of all the Indians. The dead body was sometimes placed in a pen made of sticks and covered over with bark; sometimes it was placed in a grave, and covered first with bark, and then with dirt; and sometimes, especially in the case of the young, it was placed in a rude coffin, and suspended from the top of a tree. This last was a common mode of infant burial, and the mother of the child would often be found, long after, standing under the tree, and singing songs to her babe.

Boone witnessed, too, the mode in which war-parties start off for war. The budget, or medicine-bag, is first made up. This bag contains something belonging to each man of the party—something usually representing some animal, such as the skin of a snake, the tail of a buffalo, the horns of a buck, or the feathers of a bird. It is always regarded as a very sacred thing. The leader of the party goes before with this; the rest follow in single file. When they come to a stand, the [Pg 84] budget is laid down in front, and no man may pass it without permission. To keep their thoughts upon the enterprise in which they are engaged, no man is allowed to talk of women or his home. At night, when they encamp, the heart of whatever animal has been killed during the day is cut into small pieces and then burnt. During the burning no man is allowed to step across the fire, but must always walk around it in the direction of the sun. When they spy the enemy, and the attack is to be made, the war-budget is opened. Each man takes out his budget, or *totem*, and fastens it to his body. After the fight, each man again returns his *totem* to the leader. They are all again tied up, and given to the man who has taken the first scalp. He then leads the party in triumph home.

Boone had not long been a prisoner among them when a successful war-party returned home and celebrated their victory. When the party came within a day's march of the village, a messenger was sent in to tell of their success. An order was instantly issued that every cabin should be swept clean, and the women as quickly commenced the work. When they had finished, the cabins were all inspected, to see if they were in proper order. Next day the party approached the village. They were all frightfully painted, and each man had a bunch of white feathers on his head. They were marching in single file, the chief of the party leading the way, bearing in one hand a branch of cedar, [Pg 85] laden with the scalps they had taken, and all chanting their war-song. As they entered the village, the chief led the way to the war-pole which stood in front of the council-house. In this house the council-fire was then burning. The waiter, or *Etissu* of the leader, then fixed two blocks of wood near the war-pole, and placed upon them a kind of ark, which was regarded by them as one of their most sacred things. The chief now ordered that all should sit down. He then inquired whether his cabin was prepared, and everything made ready, according to the custom of his fathers. They then rose up and commenced the war-whoop, as they marched round the war-pole. The ark was then taken and carried with great solemnity into the council-house, and here the whole party remained three days and nights, separate from the rest of the people. Their first business now was to wash themselves clean, and sprinkle themselves with a mixture of bitter herbs. While they were thus in the house, all their female relatives, after having bathed and dressed themselves in their finest clothes, placed themselves in two lines facing each other on each side of the door. Here they continued singing a slow monotonous song all day and night; the song was kept up steadily for one minute, with intervals of ten minutes of dead silence between. About once in [Pg 86] three hours the chief would march out at the head of his warriors, raise the war-whoop, and pass around the war-pole, bearing his branch of cedar. This was all that was done for the whole three days and nights. At length the purification was ended, and upon each of their cabins was placed a twig of the cedar with a fragment of the scalps fastened to it, to satisfy the ghosts of their departed friends. All were now quiet as usual, except the leader of the party and his waiter, who kept up the purification three days and nights longer. When he had finished, the budget was hung up before his door for thirty or forty days, and from time to time Indians of the party would be seen singing and dancing before it. When Boone asked the meaning of all this strange ceremony, they answered him by a word which he says meant *holy*.

As this party had brought in no prisoners, he did not now witness their horrible mode of torture. Before he left them, however, he saw enough of their awful cruelty in this way. Sometimes the poor prisoner would be tied to a stake, a pile of green wood placed around him, fire applied, and the poor wretch left to his horrible fate, while, amid shouts and yells, the Indians departed. Sometimes he would be forced to run the gauntlet between two rows of Indians, each one striking at him with a club until he fell dead. Others would be fastened between two stakes, their arms and legs stretched to each of them, and then [Pg 87] quickly burnt by a blazing fire. A common mode was to pinion the arms of the prisoner, and then tie one end of a grape-vine around his neck, while the other was fastened to the stake. A fire was then kindled, and the poor wretch would walk the circle; this gave the savages the comfort of seeing the poor creature literally roasting, while his agony was prolonged. Perhaps this was the most popular mode, too, because all the women and children could join in it. They were there, with their bundles of dry sticks, to keep the fire blazing, and their long switches, to beat the prisoner. Fearful that their victim might die too soon, and thus escape their cruelty, the women would knead cakes of clay and put them on the skull of the poor sufferer, that the fire might not reach his brain and instantly kill him. As the poor frantic wretch would run round the circle, they would yell, dance, and sing, and beat him with their switches, until he fell exhausted. At other times, a poor prisoner would be tied, and then scalding water would be poured upon him from time to time till he died. It was amazing, too, to see how the warriors would sometimes bear these tortures. Tied to the stake, they would chant their war-songs, threaten their captors with the awful vengeance of their tribe, boast of how many of their nation they had scalped and tell their tormentors how they might increase their torture. In the midst of the fire they [Pg 88] would stand unflinching, and die without changing a muscle. It was their glory to die in this way; they felt that they disappointed their enemies in their last triumph.

While Boone was with them, a noted warrior of one of the western tribes, with which the Shawanese were at war, was brought in as a captive. He was at once condemned, stripped, fastened to the stake, and the fire kindled. After suffering without flinching for a long time, he laughed at his captors, and told them they did not know how to make an enemy eat fire. He called for a pipe and tobacco. Excited by his bravery, they gave it to him. He sat down on the burning coals, and commenced smoking with the utmost composure; not a muscle of his countenance moved. Seeing this, one of his captors sprang forward and cried out that he was a true warrior. Though he had murdered many of their tribe, yet he should live, if the fire had not spoiled him. The fire had, however, well nigh done its work. With that, he declared that he was too brave a man to suffer any longer. He seized a tomahawk and raised it over the head of the prisoner: still a muscle did not move. He did not even change his posture. The blow was given, and the brave warrior fell dead.

While among them, Boone also witnessed the mode in which, the [Pg 89] Shawanese make a treaty of peace. The warriors of both tribes between which the treaty was to be made, met together first, ate and smoked in a friendly way, and then pledged themselves in a sacred drink called *cussena*. The Shawanese then waved large fans, made of eagles' tails, and danced. The other party, after this, chose six of their finest young men, painted them with white clay, and adorned their heads with swans' feathers; their leader was then placed on what was called the "consecrated seat." After this they all commenced dancing, and singing their song of peace. They danced first in a bending posture; then stood upright, still dancing, and bearing in their right hands their fans, while in their left they carried a calabash, tied to a stick about a foot long, and with this continually beat their breasts. During all this, some added to the noise by rattling pebbles in a gourd. This being over, the peace was concluded. It was an act of great solemnity, and no warrior was considered as well trained, who did not know how to join in every part of it.

Many other strange things were seen by Boone among these people, but these are enough to show you that he was among a strange people, with habits very unlike his own. It is not wonderful that he sighed to escape, when he looked upon their horrid tortures. Independently of [Pg 90] his love for Boonesborough, he did not know but that such tortures might be his at any moment, when they became excited. Fortunately, as we have seen, he did escape, and we will now go on with his story. [Pg 91]

CHAPTER VI.

WHEN Boone reached Boonesborough, the object he most loved was not to be found. His poor wife, wearied with waiting for him, and naturally concluding that he was lost to her for ever, had returned to her friends on the Yadkin. The settlers had begged her to remain, and offered her every kindness; but her husband was gone: she was heart-sick, and longed to return to her friends in Carolina. Disappointed as he was, however, he had no time to waste in sorrow. The Indians were approaching, and Boonesborough was well nigh defenceless. Just before his return, a Major Smith had taken charge of the post, and been busy in strengthening it, but much was still to be done. Boone's energies were now at work, and in a little time the station was ready for an attack. A white man now came into the [Pg 92] settlement with news. He had escaped from the Indians. The party from which Boone had escaped had postponed their attack for three weeks, and gone back to strengthen themselves. They felt that Boone had reached home—the alarm was given, the place fortified—and that it was idle to attack it at this time.

Boone determined at once to improve the mean season. With nineteen men, he started off to surprise the Indians at Paint Creek Town, a small village on the Scioto. When he came within four miles of the place, he met a party of the savages on their way to join the large body marching against Boonesborough. The fight instantly commenced: one Indian fell dead, several were wounded, and the rest were forced to retreat; their horses and all their baggage fell into the hands of Boone. Two men were now sent to reconnoitre the town. They found no Indians there; they had all left. After setting fire to the village, they returned, and Boone immediately hurried homeward.

He had scarcely entered the station, and closed the gates, when an army of four hundred and forty-four Indians, led on by a Frenchman named Duquesne, appeared before the settlement. They soon sent in a flag, demanding, in the name of the King of Great Britain, that the station should instantly surrender. A council was immediately [Pg 93] held in the fort. With such a force before them, Smith was in favor of meeting their proposal; Boone opposed it; the settlers backed him in this opposition; and he sent back for an answer to the Indians that the gates should never be opened to them. Presently another flag of truce was sent in, with a message that they had a letter for Colonel Boone from Governor Hamilton, of Detroit. Upon hearing this, it was thought best that Boone and Smith should go out and meet them, and hear what they had to say.

Fifty yards from the fort they were met by three chiefs, who received them very cordially, and led them to the spot where they were to hold the parley. Here they were seated upon a panther's skin, while the Indians held branches over their heads to protect them from the sun. The chiefs then commenced talking in a friendly way, and some of their warriors now came forward, grounded their arms, and shook hands with them. Then the letter of General Hamilton was read; he invited them to surrender and come at once to Detroit where they should be treated with all kindness. Smith objected to this proposal, declaring that it was impossible for them, at this time, to move their women and children; but the Indians had an answer ready: they had brought forty horses with them, they said, expressly to help them in removing. After a long and friendly talk, the white men returned to the fort, for the [Pg 94] purpose, as they said, of considering the proposal. They now informed the settlers that the Indians had no cannon, and advised them never to think of surrendering. Every man thought the advice good.

The Indians now sent in another flag, and asked what treaty the whites were ready to make. Boone, who had suspected treachery all the time, at once sent a reply, that if they wished to make a treaty, the place for making it, must be within sixty yards of the fort. This displeased them at first, but at last, they consented. He then stationed some of his men, with their guns, in one angle of the fort, with orders to fire if it became necessary, and, with Smith, started out to meet them. After a long talk with thirty chiefs, terms were agreed upon, and the treaty was ready to be signed; the chiefs now said that it was customary with them, on such occasions, for the Indians to shake hands with every white man who signed the treaty, as a token of the warmest friendship. Boone and Smith agreed to this, and the shaking of hands commenced; presently, they found themselves seized in the crowd—the Indians were dragging them off; a fire from the fort now levelled the savages who grasped them; the rest were in confusion, and, in the confusion, Boone and Smith escaped and rushed into the fort. In the struggle Boone was wounded, though not dangerously. [Pg 95] It was a narrow escape for both of them.

There was no more chance for deception now; the Indians were disappointed, and the whites were provoked at their treachery. A brisk firing now commenced on both sides; Duquesne harangued the Indians and urged them on, while the whites shouted from the fort, upbraided them as treacherous cowards, and defied them. The attack was furious, the firing was kept up till dark, and many an Indian fell that day before Boonesborough. The whites, sheltered by their pickets, made easy havoc among them.

When night came, the exasperated Indians crawled under the pickets and began to throw burning materials into the fort, hoping to set all on fire; but in this they were disappointed—there were ample supplies of water inside, and the fire was put out as fast as it fell.

The next day the firing was resumed, and day after day it continued, the Indians failing to make any impression. They were too far from the fort—the first day's work had taught them not to come near. At last they formed a wiser plan for doing mischief. Boonesborough, as you will remember, was only sixty yards from the river, and they determined, by the advice of the Frenchman, to let the water in and force the settlers out. In the night, they commenced the work of digging a trench under ground, from the river. In the morning Boone [Pg 96] looked out upon the river, and perceiving that it was muddy, instantly guessed the cause. He immediately set his men to the work of cutting a trench inside the fort, to cross the subterranean passage of the Indians. The savages saw what was doing, for Boone's men were constantly shovelling dirt over the pickets, but they persevered earnestly in their design. At last, however, they were forced to stop, for the dirt caved in as fast as they dug; disappointed in this, they now summoned the station once more to a treaty. But Boone laughed at them. "Do you suppose," said he, "we would pretend to treat with such treacherous wretches? Fire on, you only waste your powder; the gates shall never be opened to you while there is a man of us living." Taking his advice, they commenced their firing again; at last, on the ninth day of the siege, wearied with their fruitless labor, they killed all the cattle they could find, raised a yell, and departed. This was a terrible siege for the Indians; it is said that they lost two hundred men; Boone counted thirty-seven chief warriors; while the whites, defended by their pickets, had but two killed and four wounded. You may judge, too, how industrious the savages had been, when I tell you that the whites who wanted lead, commenced gathering their balls after they left, and succeeded in picking out of the [Pg 97] logs, and from the ground, one hundred and twenty-five pounds.

Boone having thus successfully defended his settlement, determined now to go in search of his wife. Accustomed to travelling through the woods, he soon made his lonely journey to the Yadkin. They were amazed as he entered the house of Mr. Bryan, his wife's father. The appearance of one risen from the grave could not have surprised them more than that of Boone—the lost man was among them, and great was their rejoicing. He now remained here with his family for some time, and here we will leave him for a little while, to talk of what happened in Kentucky during his absence.

The Kentuckians, roused by the Indian hostility and treachery, determined soon after he left to inflict punishment upon them; against the Shawanese they were most provoked; it was among them that most of the plots against the whites were formed, and the attack, therefore, was to be made upon them. An army of one hundred and sixty men was soon collected, and the command was given to a brave man named Colonel Bowman; they were to march directly against old Chilicothe, the den of the savages.

In July of this year (1779), they started and reached the home of the Indians, without being discovered. At daylight, the fight commenced [Pg 98] and continued till ten o'clock. Bowman's men fought bravely, but the Indians had every advantage. Knowing all the woods about their settlement, while one party fought openly, the other, concealed behind the grass and trees, poured in a deadly fire upon the whites. He was forced at last to retreat as rapidly as possible to a distance of thirty miles; but the Indians pursued him here, doing more mischief than before. The savages fought desperately. His men were falling around him, and but for Colonel Harrod, every man of them might have been killed. Seeing the slaughter that was continually increasing, he mounted a body of horsemen and made a charge upon the enemy; this broke their ranks, they were thrown into confusion, and Bowman, with the remnant of his men, was enabled to retreat.

This attack only exasperated the Indians. In the course of the next summer (after doing much mischief in a smaller way in the meantime), they gathered together to the number of six hundred, and led on by Colonel Bird, a British officer, came down upon Riddle's and Martin's stations, at the forks of Licking river. They had with them six cannons, and managed their matters so secretly, that the first news of their approach was given to the settlers by the roar of their guns. Of course it was of no use to resist; the pickets could not defend them from cannon-balls; the settlers were [Pg 99] forced to surrender. The savages rushed into the station and instantly killed one man and two women with their tomahawks; all the others, many of whom were sick, were now loaded with baggage and forced to march off with the Indians. It was certain death to any one, old or young, male or female, who became, on the march, too weak and exhausted to travel farther; they were instantly killed with the tomahawk.

Flushed with success, the Indians were now more troublesome than ever; it was impossible for the whites to remain in the country if matters were to go on in this way. The inhabitants at last threw themselves upon the protection of Colonel Clarke, who commanded a regiment of United States soldiers at the falls of the Ohio. At the head of his men and a large number of volunteers, he marched against Pecaway, one of the principal towns of the Shawanese; numbers of the savages were killed, and the town was burnt to ashes. This was a triumph, but it was a triumph gained by the loss of seventeen of his men.

In 1780, Boone again returned to Boonesborough with his family, bringing with him also a younger brother. The elder brother (who had been in Kentucky before, as you will remember) now returned also, and made his home at a spot not far from the place where the town of Shelbyville now stands. The settlers were all delighted to see [Pg 100] their old friend Daniel Boone once more among them; they now felt that their leader was on the ground. Mrs. Boone too felt happy. Though she was again on "*the dark and bloody ground,*" her husband was with her.

In a little time his services were again especially needed. The want of salt, their old trouble was upon them, and they looked to Boone to procure it. Ever ready, he started off with his younger brother to the Blue Licks, the place of his former trouble; here he was destined to meet with trouble again. They had made as much salt as they could carry, and were now returning to Boonesborough with their packs, when they were suddenly overtaken by a party of savages; the Indians immediately fired, and Boone's brother fell dead. Daniel Boone turned, levelled his rifle at the foremost Indian, and brought him down; with a loud yell the party now rushed toward him. He snatched his brother's rifle, levelled another, and then ran. The Indians gave chase, but he managed to keep ahead, and even found time to reload his rifle. He knew that his only chance for escape was to distance them, and break his trail. He passed the brow of a hill, jumped into a brook below, waded in it for some distance, and then struck off at right angles from his old course. Upon looking back he found, to his sorrow, that he had not succeeded—the Indians were still on [Pg 101] his track. Presently, he came to a grape-vine, and tried his old experiment at breaking the trail. This was to no purpose, he found the savages still following him. After travelling some distance farther, upon looking round he saw the cause of his trouble; the Indians had a dog with them, and this dog, scenting his track, kept them for ever on his course. His rifle was loaded—the dog was far ahead of the party—and Boone sent a rifle ball through him. He now pushed on, doubling his course from time to time; the Indians lost track of him, and he reached Boonesborough in safety.

In spite of the continued annoyance of the Indians, the white settlements had continued to grow, and there were now so many white men in the country, that in the fall of this year (1780), Kentucky was divided into the three counties of Jefferson, Fayette, and Lincoln. Our friend, Daniel Boone, was appointed to command the militia in his county, and William Pope, and Benjamin Logan, two brave men, were to have the command in theirs.

The winter of this year soon set in, and it proved a hard one. The settlers, however, bore it cheerfully, for they were accustomed to hardships. Hard as it was, too, it proved mild to the next that followed. The winter of 1781 was long remembered as "the cold winter" in Kentucky. To make it harder, the Indians, after doing much mischief through the summer, had destroyed most of the crops the preceding [Pg 102] fall, and the settlers had small supplies of food. But the forest was around them; Boone and Harrod were among them, and these two men found food enough. Every day they went out in the winter's storms—every night they came in laden with deer and buffaloes. The people learned to live on nothing but meat. Boone and Harrod drove away all thoughts of starvation. They had, however, this one comfort: the cold weather kept the Indians at home. They had no disturbances throughout the winter from them.

When spring opened, however, the savages showed themselves more furious, if possible, than ever. Their plans of mischief were better laid; they seemed to have been feeding their revenge fat. Open and secret war was all around the settlers. It would be idle for me to attempt to give details of the doings of the savages. Ashton's, Hoy's, M'Afee's, Kincheloe's, and Boone's station, near Shelbyville, were all attacked. Men were shot down in the open fields, or waylaid in every pathway. The early annals of Kentucky are filled with stories of many a brave white man at this time. There were Ashton, Holden, Lyn, Tipton, Chapman, White, Boone, Floyd, Wells, the M'Afees, M'Gary, Randolph, Reynolds, and others, some of whom were killed, and all of whom had their hard struggles. The history of that spring is only a story of burnings, captures, and murders, on the part of the savages. [Pg 103] It was a dark period for the white men; even Boone, with all his vigor and fearlessness, thought it the darkest period he had known in that region. The savages seemed bent upon a war of extermination.

Not satisfied with such mischief as they had already done, in the early part of the summer the savages held a grand council at Old Chilicothe, to arrange their plans for further destruction. There were chiefs there from the Cherokees, Wyandots, Tawas, Pottawattomies, and most of the tribes bordering on the lakes. Two notorious white villains—whose names will never be forgotten in Kentucky—were there also, to aid them with their counsels. These were Girty and

M'Kee, infamous men, who lived among the Indians, and lived only by murdering their own countrymen. Their plan was soon settled. Bryant's station, near Lexington, was known to be a strong post, and this was to be attacked. This station had within it forty cabins, and here it was thought they might make the greatest slaughter. The warriors were to gather as rapidly as possible for the enterprise.

In a little time, five hundred of them rallied at Girty's cabin, ready for their departure. The white rascal then made a speech to them. He told them that "Kentucky was a beautiful hunting-ground, filled with deer and buffaloes, for their comfort; the white men had come to drive [Pg 104] them away; the ground was now red with the blood of the red men that had been slain. But vengeance they would have—now, before the whites were yet fastened in the country, they would strike a blow, and drive them off for ever." Then he talked of the plan before them. He advised them to descend the Miami in their canoes, cross the Ohio, ascend the Licking, and then they might paddle their boats almost to the station. His speech was answered by a loud yell from the Indians, and they all started off for their boats—Simon Girty, with his ruffled shirt and soldier coat, marching at their head.

On the night of the 15th of August, they arrived before the station. In the morning, as the gates were opened, the men were fired at by the savages, and this was the first news to the whites of the approach of the enemy. It was fortunate that they had shown themselves thus early: in two hours more, most of the men were to have started off to aid a distant feeble station. As soon as the whites found they were besieged, they managed to send off the news to Lexington.

The Indians now, as usual, commenced their stratagems. The large body concealed themselves in the grass near the pathway to the spring, while one hundred went round and attacked the south-east angle of the station. Their hope was to draw the whites all to that quarter, while they forced an entrance on the other side. But the white men [Pg 105] understood this sort of cunning; they had lived among the Indians too long to be caught by such tricks: instead of noticing the attack, they went on quietly with the work of repairing and strengthening their palisades.

But water, one of the necessaries of life, was soon wanting. The whites, as they looked at the tall grass and weeds near the spring, felt that Indians were lurking there. The women now came forward and insisted upon it that they would go and bring water. "What if they do shoot us?" they said; "it is better to lose a woman than a man at such a time." With that, they started out, and, strange to tell, went back and forth, bringing supplies of water, without any difficulty. Some of the young men now went out upon the same purpose. They had scarcely left the station, when they were fired upon. Fortunately, the Indians were too far to do any mischief; the men retreated rapidly within the palisades. The Indians, finding their stratagem fruitless, now rushed forward, and commenced a tremendous attack. The whites received them with a steady fire, and many of them fell. Enraged the more, they now discharged their burning arrows into the roofs of the houses; some of the cabins were burnt, but an east wind was blowing at the time, and that saved the station. [Pg 106]

The enemy now fell back into the grass. They had found out, in some way, that help was expected from Lexington, and they were preparing to cut it off. In a little time, all was still. Presently sixteen horsemen, followed by thirty-one foot-soldiers, were seen coming; these were the men from Lexington. Thinking only of the distress of their friends, they were hurrying along, when the Indians opened a fire upon them. The horsemen galloped off in a cloud of dust, and reached the station in safety. The soldiers on foot, in their effort to escape, plunged into the cornfields on either side of the road, only to meet the enemy. A desperate fight commenced on both sides: two soldiers were killed; the rest—four of them having dangerous wounds—reached the pickets. The exasperated Indians, disappointed at the escape of this party, now wreaked their vengeance by killing all the cattle they could find.

Finding all their efforts to enter the station idle, Simon Girty now came near enough to be heard, mounted a stump, and holding in his hand a flag of truce, began to talk. "Surrender promptly," cried Simon; "if you surrender promptly, no blood shall be shed; but if you will not surrender, then know that our cannons and reinforcements are coming. We will batter down your pickets as we did at Riddle's and Martin's; every man of you shall be slain; two are dead already four are [Pg 107] wounded; every man shall die." This language was so insolent, that some of the settlers cried out, "Shoot the rascal!" No man, however, lifted his rifle; the flag of truce protected him. "I am under a flag of truce," cried Simon; "do you know who it is that speaks to you?"

Upon this, a young man named Reynolds leaped up and cried out, "Know you! know you! yes, we know you well. Know Simon Girty! yes: he is the renegado, cowardly villain, who loves to murder women and children, especially those of his own people. Know Simon Girty! yes: his father must have been a panther, and his mother a wolf. I have a worthless dog that kills lambs: instead of shooting him, I have named him Simon Girty. You expect reinforcements and cannon, do you? Cowardly wretches like you, that make war upon women and children, would not dare to touch them off, if you had them. We expect reinforcements, too, and in numbers to give a short account of the murdering cowards that follow you. Even if you could batter down our pickets, I, for one, hold your people in too much contempt to shoot rifles at them. I would not waste powder and ball upon you. Should you even enter our fort, I am ready for you; I have roasted a number of hickory switches, with which we mean to whip you and your naked cut-throats out of the country!" [Pg 108]

Simon was now furious; cursing and swearing, he went back to his friends, amid the loud laughs and jeers of the whites. In a little time, the firing was renewed; it was all to no purpose: no white man suffered, and every Indian who came within gun-shot of the fort was sure to fall. In the course of the night the whole party sneaked off, and their tracks indicated that they had started for the Blue Licks. They left behind them thirty of their number slain. [Pg 109]

CHAPTER VII.

COLONEL TODD, of Lexington, instantly despatched news of this attack on Bryant's station, to Colonel Boone, at Boonesborough, and Colonel Trigg, near Harrodsburgh. In a little time, one hundred and seventy-six men were collected under these three officers, to march in pursuit. Majors M'Gary and Harland now joined them, determined that they would have a part in the punishment of the savages. It was known, too, that Colonel Logan was collecting a force, and a council of officers was at once held, to determine whether they should march on, or wait for him. They were all so eager to be off, that it was thought best to march immediately. The march was therefore commenced forthwith. [Pg 110]

Following on in the trail of the Indians, they had not gone far, when Boone saw enough to convince him that the Indians would not only be willing, but glad to meet them. No effort had been made to conceal their trail; the trees were even marked on their pathway, that the whites might follow on; and they had tried to conceal their numbers, by treading in each other's footsteps. He called the attention of his companions to this, but still they proceeded onward.

They saw no Indians until they came to the Licking river, not far from the Blue Licks. A party was now seen on the other side of the stream, leisurely crossing a hill. A council was at once held, and the officers all turned to Boone for advice. His advice was given frankly: he was for waiting till Logan should arrive with his men. The Indian party, he felt assured, was at the least from four to five hundred strong, and the unconcerned mode in which the Indians crossed the hill showed that the main body was near, and their design was to draw them over the river. Moreover, he was acquainted with all that region of the country. After they crossed the ford, they would come upon deep ravines not far from the bank, where, no doubt, the Indians were in ambush. If, however, they were determined not to wait for Logan, he advised that the country might at least be reconnoitred before the attack was made. A part of the men, he thought, might cross the [Pg 111] stream, and move up cautiously on the other side, while the remainder would stand where they were, ready to assist them at the first alarm. Todd and Trigg thought the advice good, and were disposed to heed it; but, just at this moment, Major M'Gary, more hot-headed than wise, spurred his horse into the water, gave the Kentucky war-whoop, and cried out, "All those that are not cowards will follow me; I will show them where the Indians are." The men were roused by this show of bravery, and they all crossed the ford.

The banks were steep on the other side, and many of them now dismounted, tied their horses, and commenced marching on foot. M'Gary and Harland led the way. They had not proceeded far when they came to one of the ravines. It was just as Boone had supposed; the savages were in ambush. A deadly fire was now poured in upon the whites; the men staggered and fell in every direction. The fire was returned, but to little purpose, for the enemy was completely concealed; a retreat was all that was left. The whites hurried back toward the river; the Indians pursued; and now commenced the slaughter with the tomahawk. The ford was narrow, and multitudes were slaughtered there. Some were trying to get to their horses; others, more fortunate, were mounted and flying; and some were plunging into the stream. In the midst of [Pg 112] all this confusion, the Indians were doing their work of destruction.

A man by the name of Netherland (who had been laughed at for his cowardice) had never dismounted his horse, and was the first to reach the opposite shore. In a little time, some of his comrades were around him. He now turned, and, looking back, saw the massacre that was going on. This was more than he could bear. "Halt! fire on the Indians," cried he; "protect the men in the river." With this, the men wheeled, fired, and rescued several poor fellows in the stream, over whom the tomahawk was lifted.

Reynolds, the man who answered Girty's insolence, made a narrow escape. Finding, in the retreat, one of the officers wounded, he gave him his horse, and was soon after taken by three Indians. They were now over him, ready to despatch him, when two retreating white men rushed by. Two of the savages started in pursuit; the third stooped for an instant to tie his moccasin, when Reynolds sprang away from him and escaped.

This was a terrible battle for the white men. More than sixty of their number were slain, and among them were most of their officers: Colonels Todd and Trigg, Majors Harland and Bulger, Captains Gordon and M'Bride, and a son of Colonel Boone, were all among the dead. [Pg 113]

Those who had regained the other shore, not having strength to rally, started homeward in great sadness. On their way they met Colonel Logan. He had gone to Bryant's station with his five hundred men, and was greatly disappointed when he found they had all started without him; he pushed on, however, as rapidly as he could, hoping to overtake them before they made their attack on the savages. The sad story of the defeat was soon told. All that remained to be done now was to go back, and, if possible, bury the dead. Upon this sad business Logan continued his march. Upon reaching the ground, the spectacle was awful: the dead bodies were strewn over it just as they had fallen, the heat was intense, and birds of prey were feeding upon the carcasses. The bodies were so mangled and changed, that no man could be distinguished; friends could not recognise their nearest relatives. The dead were buried as rapidly as possible, and Logan left the scene in great sorrow.

Nor was this all the carnage. The Indians, after the defeat, had scattered, and it was soon found that on their way homeward they had swept through several settlements, carrying destruction before them. Emboldened by their triumph, no man could tell what they might next attempt.

It was no time for the whites to be idle. They soon rallied in large numbers at Fort Washington, the present site of the city of [Pg 114] Cincinnati. General Clarke was at once made commander-in-chief, and Colonel Logan was placed next under him in command. Clarke immediately started with a thousand men to attack the Indian towns on the Miami. On his way he came upon the cabin of Simon Girty; it was fortunate for Simon that a straggling Indian spied Clarke's men coming, in time to let him escape. The news was now spread everywhere that an army of white men was coming from Kentucky. The consequence was, that as Clarke approached the towns, he found them all deserted; the Indians had fled to the woods. His march, however, was not made for nothing. The towns of Old and New Chilicothe, Pecaway, and Wills' Town, were all reduced to ashes. One old Indian warrior was surprised, and surrendered himself a prisoner. This man, to the great sorrow of General Clarke, was afterward murdered by one of the soldiers.

Notwithstanding this punishment, Indian massacres still went on. Stories of savage butchery were heard of everywhere; every station that they dared approach felt their fury, and the poor settler who had built his cabin away from any station was sure to be visited.

General Clarke started out again, against the Indians on the Wabash. Unfortunately, his expedition failed this time, for the want of provisions for [Pg 115] his men. Another expedition of Colonel Logan, against the Shawanese Indians, was more successful. He surprised one of their towns, killed many of their warriors, and took many prisoners.

The war had now become so serious, that in the fall of 1785 the General Government invited all the lake and Ohio tribes of Indians to meet at the mouth of the Great Miami. It was hoped that in this way matters might be settled peaceably. But many of the tribes were insolent and ill-natured; they refused to come in, giving as an excuse that the Kentuckians were for ever molesting them. Emboldened by the very invitation, they continued the warfare more vigorously than ever. They not only assaulted the settlements already made, but made an attempt to guard the Ohio river, to prevent any further settlers from reaching the country in that direction. Small parties placed themselves at different points on the river, from Pittsburgh to Louisville, where they laid in ambush and fired upon every boat that passed. Sometimes they would make false signals, decoy the boat ashore, and murder the whole crew. They even went so far at last as to arm and man the boats they had taken, and cruise up and down the river.

I must tell you of a very bold defence made on the Ohio about this time by a Captain Hubbel, who was bringing a party of emigrants from [Pg 116] Vermont. His party was in two boats, and consisted in all of twenty. As Hubbel came down the river, he fell in with other boats, was told of the Indian stratagems, and advised to be careful. Indeed, the inmates of some of the boats begged that he would continue in their company, and thus they would be able to meet the Indians better if they should be attacked; the stronger the party, the better, in such a condition. But Hubbel refused to do this, and proceeded onward. He had not gone far, when a man on the shore began to make signs of distress, and begged that the boat might come and take him off. Hubbel knew well enough that this was an Indian disguised as a white man, and therefore took no notice of him. In a little time, a party of savages pushed off in their boats, and attacked him fiercely. The fight was hot on both sides. The savages tried to board Hubbel's boat, but the fire was too hot for this. Hubbel received two severe wounds, and had the lock of his gun shot off by an Indian; still he fought, touching off his broken gun from time to time with a firebrand. The Indians found the struggle too hard, and were glad to paddle off. Presently they returned, and attacked the other boat; this they seized almost without an effort, killed the captain and a boy, and took all the women as prisoners to their own boats. Now they came once more against Hubbel, and cunningly placed the women on the sides of their boats as a sort [Pg 117] of bulwark. But this did not stop Hubbel: he saw that his balls must strike the women; but it was better that they should be killed now, rather than suffer a death of torture from the savages, and the fire was at once opened upon them again. They were soon driven off once more. In the course of the action, however, Hubbel's boat drifted near the shore, and five hundred savages renewed the fire upon them. One of the emigrants, more imprudent than the rest, seeing a fine chance for a shot, raised his head to take aim, and was instantly killed by a ball. The boat drifted along, and at length reached deep water again. It was then found, that of the nine men on board, two only had escaped unhurt; two were killed, and two mortally wounded. A remarkable lad on board showed great courage. He now asked his friends to extract a ball that had lodged in the skin of his forehead; and when this was done, he begged that they would take out a piece of bone that had been fractured in his elbow by another ball. His poor frightened mother, seeing his suffering, asked him why he had not complained before; to which the little fellow replied that he had been too busy, and, besides that, the captain had told them all to make no noise.

It was idle to attempt now to settle matters peaceably. The general government had tried that and the plan had failed. The war was now [Pg 118] to be carried on to a close, come what might. An expedition was accordingly planned, against all the tribes northwest of the Ohio. The Indians were to be brought out, if possible to a general fight; or, if that could not be done, all their towns and cabins on the Scioto and Wabash, were to be destroyed. General Harmar was appointed commander of the main expedition, and Major Hamtranck was to aid him with a smaller party.

In the fall of 1791, Harmar started from Fort Washington with three hundred and twenty men. In a little time he was joined by the Kentucky and Pennsylvania militia, so that his whole force now amounted to fourteen hundred and fifty-three men. Colonel Hardin, who commanded the Kentucky militia, was now sent ahead with six hundred men, principally militia, to reconnoitre the country. Upon reaching the Indian settlements, the savages set fire to their houses and fled; to overtake them, he pushed on with two hundred of his men. A party of Indians met and attacked them. The cowardly militia ran off, leaving their brave companions to be slaughtered. It was a brave struggle, but almost all were cut down; only seven managed to escape and join the main army.

Harmar felt deeply mortified. He commenced forthwith his return to Fort Washington, but determined that, on the way, he would wipe off this disgrace from his army. Upon coming near Chilicothe [Pg 119] he accordingly halted, and in the night despatched Colonel Hardin once more ahead, with orders to find the enemy and draw them into an engagement. About daybreak, Hardin came upon them, and the battle commenced. It was a desperate fight on both sides. Some of the militia acted badly again, but the officers behaved nobly. The victory was claimed on both sides, but I think the Indians had the best of it. Three gallant officers, Fontaine, Willys, and Frothingham, were slain, together with fifty regulars and one hundred militia.

Harmar now moved on to Fort Washington. So much was said about his miserable campaign, that he requested that he might be tried by a court-martial. Accordingly he was tried and honorably acquitted.

A new army was soon raised, and the command was now given to Major-General Arthur St. Clair. His plan was to destroy the Indian settlements between the Miamies, drive the savages from that region, and establish a chain of military posts there, which should for ever keep them out of the country. All having rallied at Fort Washington, he started off in the direction of the Miami towns. It was a hard march, for he was forced to cut his roads as he passed along. Upon arriving near the Indian country, he built forts Hamilton and Jefferson and garrisoned them. This left him nearly two thousand men to proceed with. In a little time some of the worthless militia [Pg 120] deserted. This was a bad example to the rest, and St. Clair instantly sent Major Hamtranck, with a regiment, in pursuit of them, while he continued his march. When he arrived within fifteen miles of the Miami villages he halted and encamped; he was soon after joined by Major Hamtranck, and St. Clair proposed now immediately to march against the enemy.

But the enemy had already got news of them, and had made ready. They were determined to have the first blow themselves. At daybreak the next morning, the savages attacked the militia and drove them back in confusion. These broke through the regulars, forcing their way into the camp, the Indians pressing hard on their heels. The officers tried to restore order, but to no purpose: the fight now became general. This, however, was only a small part of the Indian force—there were four thousand of the party; they had nearly surrounded the camp, and sheltered by the trees and grass as usual, were pouring in a deadly fire upon the whites. St. Clair and all his officers behaved with great courage. Finding his men falling fast around him, he ordered a charge to be made with the bayonet. The men swept through the long grass driving the Indians before them. The charge had no sooner ceased than the Indians returned. Some forced their way into the camp, killed the artillerists, wounded Colonel Butler, and seized the cannon. [Pg 121] Wounded as he was, Butler drove them back and recovered the guns. Fired with new ardor, they returned again, once more entered the camp—once more had possession of the cannon. All was now confusion among the whites—it was impossible to restore order—the Indians brought them down in masses—a retreat was all that remained. But they were so hemmed in, that this seemed impossible. Colonel Darke was ordered to charge the savages behind them, while Major Clarke with his battalion was commanded to cover the rear of the army. These orders were instantly obeyed, and the disorderly retreat commenced. The Indians pursued them four miles, keeping up a running fight. At last their chief, a Mississago, who had been trained to war by the British, cried out to them to stop as they had killed enough. They then returned to plunder the camp and divide the spoils, while the routed troops continued their flight to Fort Jefferson, throwing away their arms on the roadside that they might run faster. The Indians found in the camp seven pieces of cannon, two hundred oxen, and several horses, and had a great rejoicing. Well might the Mississago chief tell his people they had killed enough: thirty-eight commissioned officers were slain, and five hundred and ninety-three non-commissioned officers and privates. Besides this, twenty-one officers and two hundred and [Pg 122] forty-two men were wounded, some of whom soon died of their wounds.

This was a most disastrous battle for the whites, the most disastrous they had yet known. The triumphant Indians were so delighted that they could not leave the field, but kept up their revels from day to day. Their revels, however, were at length broken up sorrowfully for them. General Scott, hearing of the disaster, pushed on for the field with one thousand mounted volunteers from Kentucky. The Indians were dancing and singing, and riding the horses and oxen in high glee. Scott instantly attacked them; two hundred were killed, their plunder retaken, and the whole body of savages driven from the ground.

When Congress met soon after this, of course this wretched Indian war was much talked of. It was proposed at once to raise three additional regiments. Upon this a hot debate sprang up, the proposal was opposed warmly; the opponents said that it would be necessary to lay a heavy tax upon the people to raise them, that the war had been badly managed, and should have been trusted to the militia in the west under their own officers, and, moreover, that no success could be expected so long as the British continued to hold posts in our own limits, and furnish the Indians with arms, ammunition, and advice.

On the other hand, it was declared that the war was a just and [Pg 123] necessary one. It was shown that in seven years (between 1783 and 1790), fifteen hundred people in Kentucky had been murdered or taken captives by the savages; while in Pennsylvania and Virginia matters had been well nigh as bad; that everything had been done to settle matters peaceably but all to no purpose. In 1790, when a treaty was proposed to the Indians of the Miami, they asked for thirty days to deliberate—the request was granted—during those thirty days one hundred and twenty persons had been killed or captured, and at the end of the time the savages refused to give any answer to the proposal. At last the vote was taken—the resolution passed—the war was to be carried on—the regiments were to be raised.

General St. Clair now resigned the command of the army, and Major General Anthony Wayne was appointed to succeed him. This appointment gave great joy to the western people; the man was so well known among them for his daring and bravery, that he commonly went by the name of "Mad Anthony."

After much delay, the regiments were at last gathered together. Some still opposed this war and in order to prove to them that the government was willing to settle matters peaceably, if possible, two officers—Colonel Hardin and Major Truman, were now sent off to the Indians with proposals of peace. They were both seized and murdered by the savages. [Pg 124]

Wayne now started out upon his expedition. In a little time he passed Fort Jefferson, took possession of St. Clair's fatal field, and erected a fort there which he called Fort Recovery. He now learned the truth of the stories about the British. A number of British soldiers had come down from Detroit, and fortified themselves on the Miami of the lakes. It was rumored too, that in some of the Indian fights and massacres, the English were seen among them, fighting and urging them on.

[Pg 125] The General continued his march, and early in August reached the confluence of the Miami of the Lakes and the Au Glaize. This was one of the finest countries of the Indians, it was about thirty miles from the British post, and he discovered here, that two thousand warriors were near that post ready to meet him. Wayne was glad to hear this; his army was quite as strong, and he longed to meet the savages. As he drew near, however, he determined once more to have peace if possible, without shedding blood. A message was sent to the Indians, urging them not to follow the advice of bad men, to lay down their arms, to learn to live peaceably, and their lives and their homes should be protected by the government. An insolent answer, was all that was received in reply.

Wayne's army now marched on in columns—a select battalion, under Major Price, moving in front to reconnoitre. After marching about five miles, Price was driven back by the fire of the Indians. As usual, the cunning enemy was concealed; they had hid themselves in a thick wood a little in advance of the British post, and here Price had received their fire.

Wayne had now found out precisely where they were, and gave his orders accordingly. The cavalry under Captain Campbell were commanded to enter the wood in the rear of the Indians, between them and the river, and charge their left flank. General Scott, with eleven hundred mounted Kentucky volunteers, was to make a circuit in the opposite direction, and attack the right. The infantry were to advance with trailed arms, and rouse the enemy from their hiding-places. All being ready, the infantry commenced their march. The Indians were at once routed at the point of the bayonet. The infantry had done the whole; Campbell and Scott had hardly the chance of doing any of the fighting. In the course of an hour, they had driven the savages back two miles; in fact, within gun-shot of the British post.

Wayne had now the possession of the whole ground, and here he remained three days, burning their houses and cornfields above and below the fort. One Englishman suffered, too, in this work of destruction. [Pg 126] Colonel M'Kee was known as a British trader, forever instigating the Indians against the Americans, and Wayne did not scruple to burn all his houses and stores likewise. Major Campbell, who commanded the British fort, remonstrated at this, but Wayne gave him a bold and determined answer in reply, and he had no more to say. A few words from him would only have caused Wayne to drive him from the country.

The army now returned to Au Glaize, destroying all the houses, villages, and crops by the way. It was one complete work of destruction; within fifty miles of the river everything was destroyed. In this campaign, Wayne had lost one hundred and seven men, and among them were two brave officers—Captain Campbell and Lieutenant Towles, but still he had gained a glorious victory. In his track, too, he had not forgotten to build forts, to guard against the savages in future.

The story of the victory soon spread, and struck terror to the hearts of the Indians north and south. They were restless and dissatisfied, but war was sure destruction to them; they felt that it was idle to attempt it further, and were ready to be quiet. In less than a year from this time, Wayne concluded a treaty, in behalf of the United States with all the Indian tribes northwest of the Ohio. The settlers at last had peace—a blessing which they had long desired. [Pg 127]

CHAPTER VIII.

WITH the return of peace, the settlers were very happy. They could now go out, fell the forests, and cultivate their fields in safety. There was no longer any wily savage to lay in ambush, and keep them in perpetual anxiety. No man among them was happier than Boone. He had been harassed by constant struggles ever since he came to Kentucky, and these struggles with the savages had made him a warrior rather than a hunter; but he could now return to his darling passion. While others cultivated the ground, he roamed through the wilderness with his rifle; he was now a hunter indeed, spending weeks and months uninterruptedly in the forests By day he moved where he pleased, and at night made his camp fearlessly wherever the shades of night overtook him. His life was now happier than ever. [Pg 128]

Ere long, however, a cloud came over this happiness. Men began again to crowd too closely upon him. In spite of all the early struggles with the savages in Kentucky, emigrants had continued to flow into that country. As early as 1783, Kentucky had been laid off into three counties, and was that year formed into one district, and called the District of Kentucky. In 1785, a convention was called at Danville, and a memorial was addressed to the legislature of Virginia, proposing that Kentucky should be erected into an independent State. In 1786, the legislature of Virginia took the necessary steps for making the new State, if Congress would admit it into the Union. In 1792, Kentucky was admitted into the Union as one of the United States of America. And now that peace had come to aid the settlers, emigration flowed in more rapidly. Court-houses, jails, judges, lawyers, sheriffs, and constables, began necessarily to be seen. Kentucky was becoming every day a more settled and civilized region, and Boone's heart grew sick. He had sought the wilderness, and men were fast taking it away from him. He began to think of moving.

Another sorrow now came over him, and soon fixed in him the determination to seek a new home. Men began to dispute with him the [Pg 129] title to his land. The State of Kentucky had not been surveyed by the government, and laid off into sections and townships, as the lands north of the Ohio river have since been. The government of Virginia had issued certificates, entitling the holder to locate where he pleased the number of acres called for. To actual settlers, who should build a cabin, raise a crop, &c., pre-emption rights to such lands as they might occupy were also granted. Entries of these certificates were made in a way so loose, that different men frequently located the same lands; one title would often lap over upon another; and almost all the titles conferred in this way became known as "the lapping, or shingle titles." Continued lawsuits sprang out of this state of things; no man knew what belonged to him. Boone had made these loose entries of his lands: his titles, of course, were disputed. It was curious to see the old man in a court of law, which he thoroughly despised, fighting for his rights. He was greatly provoked; he had explored and redeemed the wilderness, as he said, borne every hardship with his wife and children, only to be cheated at last. But the law decided against him; he lost his lands, and would now no longer remain in that region.

Hearing that buffaloes and deer were still plenty about the Great Kanhawa river, he started thither with his wife and children, and [Pg 130] settled near Point Pleasant. Here he remained several years. He was disappointed in not finding game as he expected, and was more of a farmer here than ever before; he turned his attention earnestly to agriculture, and was very successful in raising good crops. Still he was dissatisfied; he longed for the wilderness. Hunting and trapping were the constant thoughts of his life.

While living here, he met accidentally with a party of men who had been out upon the upper waters of the Missouri. These men talked of the beauty of that region: they had stories to tell of grizzly bears, buffaloes, deer, beavers, and otters—in fact, the region was in their eyes "the paradise for a hunter." Fired by these stories, Boone resolved to go there. Accordingly, he gathered together all that he possessed, and with his wife and family started for Missouri, driving his herds and cattle before him. It was strange to see an old man thus vigorous in seeking a new home. He was an object of surprise to every one. When he reached Cincinnati, on his route, some one, marking his age, and surprised at his adventure, asked him how, at his time of life, he could leave all the comforts of home, for the wilderness. His answer shows his whole character: "Too much crowded, too much crowded," said he; "I want more elbow-room." Travelling on, he at [Pg 131] length reached Missouri, and, proceeding about fifty miles above St. Louis, settled in what is now St. Charles county.

Here everything pleased Boone. The country, as you know, was then in the possession of the French and Spanish, and the old laws by which their territories were governed were still in force there. They had no constitution, no king, no legislature, no judges, lawyers, or sheriffs. An officer called the commandant, and the priests, exercised all the authority that was needed. The horses, cattle, flocks, and herds of these people all grazed together upon the same commons; in fact, they were living here almost in primitive simplicity. Boone's character for honesty and courage soon became known among them, and he was appointed by the Spanish commandant the commandant over the district of St. Charles.

Boone now had the satisfaction of settling all his children comfortably around him, and in the unbroken wilderness his hunting and trapping was unmolested. In his office of commandant he gave great satisfaction to every one, and continued to occupy it until Missouri was purchased by our government from the French. When that purchase was made, American enterprise soon came upon him again—he was once more crowded by his fellow-men. His old office of commandant was soon merged in the new order of things—his hunting-grounds were invaded by [Pg 132] others. Nothing remained for him now, but to submit to his fate; he was too old to move again, nor indeed did he know where to go. He continued his old habits, as well he might. He would start out with his rifle, now marked with a paper sight to guide his dim eye, and be absent from his home for weeks. Nearly eighty years had passed over him, yet he would lie in wait near the salt-licks, and bring down his buffalo or his deer, and as bravely and cheerily as in his younger days, would he cut down bee-trees. As the light-hearted Frenchmen swept up the river in their fleets of periogues on their hunting excursions, Boone would cheer them as they passed, and sigh for his younger days that he might join their parties. He was a complete Nimrod, now almost worn out.

It was while he was living here, I think, that he was met by that very interesting man, Mr. Audubon, the natural historian of our continent. He was struck with the man, and has given the story of his interview with Boone. It is so illustrative of the character of the hunter, that I give it to you in Mr. Audubon's words.

"Daniel Boone, or as he was usually called in the western country, Colonel Boone, happened to spend a night under the same roof with me, more than twenty years ago. We had returned from a shooting excursion, in the course of which his extraordinary skill in the management of a [Pg 133] rifle had been fully displayed. On retiring to the room appropriated to that remarkable individual and myself for the night, I felt anxious to know more of his exploits and adventures than I did, and accordingly took the liberty of proposing numerous questions to him. The stature and general appearance of this wanderer of the western forests, approached the gigantic. His chest was broad and prominent; his muscular powers displayed themselves in every limb; his countenance gave indication of his great courage, enterprise, and perseverance; and when he spoke, the very motion of his lips brought the impression, that whatever he uttered could not be otherwise than strictly true. I undressed, while he merely took off his hunting shirt, and arranged a few folds of blankets on the floor; choosing rather to lie there, as he observed, than on the softest bed. When we had both disposed of ourselves, each after his own fashion, he related to me the following account of his powers of memory, which I lay before you, kind reader, in his own words, hoping that the simplicity of his style may prove interesting to you.

"I was once," said he, "on a hunting expedition on the banks of the Green river, when the lower parts of this (Kentucky) were still in the hands of nature, and none but the sons of the soil were looked upon as its lawful proprietors. We Virginians had for some time been waging a [Pg 134] war of intrusion upon them, and I, among the rest, rambled through the woods, in pursuit of their race, as I now would follow the tracks of any ravenous animal. The Indians outwitted me one dark night, and I was as unexpectedly as suddenly made a prisoner by them. The trick had been managed with great skill; for no sooner had I extinguished the fire of my camp, and laid me down to rest, in full security, as I thought, than I felt myself seized by an indistinguishable number of hands, and was immediately pinioned, as if about to be led to the scaffold for execution. To have attempted to be refractory, would have proved useless and dangerous to my life; and I suffered myself to be removed from my camp to theirs, a few miles distant, without uttering even a word of complaint. You are aware, I dare say, that to act in this manner, was the best policy, as you understand that by so doing, I proved to the Indians at once, that I was born and bred as fearless of death as any of themselves.

"When we reached the camp, great rejoicings were exhibited. Two squaws, and a few papooses, appeared particularly delighted at the sight of me, and I was assured, by very unequivocal gestures and words, that, on the morrow, the mortal enemy of the red-skins would cease to live. I never opened my lips, but was busy contriving some scheme which might enable me to give the rascals the slip before [Pg 135] dawn. The women immediately fell a searching about my hunting-shirt for whatever they might think valuable, and fortunately for me, soon found my flask, filled with *Monongahela* (that is, reader, strong whiskey). A terrific grin was exhibited on their murderous countenances, while my heart throbbed with joy at the anticipation of their intoxication. The crew immediately began to beat their bellies and sing, as they passed the bottle from mouth to mouth. How often did I wish the flask ten times its size, and filled with aquafortis! I observed that the squaws drank more freely than the warriors, and again my spirits were about to be depressed, when the report of a gun was heard at a distance. The Indians all jumped on their feet. The singing and drinking were both brought to a stand; and I saw with inexpressible joy, the men walk off to some distance, and talk to the squaws. I knew that they were consulting about me, and I foresaw, that in a few moments the warriors would go to discover the cause of the gun having been fired so near their camp. I expected the squaws would be left to guard me. Well, sir, it was just so. They returned; the men took up their guns and walked away. The squaws sat down again, and in less than five minutes they had my bottle up to their dirty mouths, gurgling down their throats the remains of the whiskey. [Pg 136]

"With what pleasure did I see them becoming more and more drunk, until the liquor took such hold of them that it was quite impossible for these women to be of any service. They tumbled down, rolled about, and began to snore; when I, having no other chance of freeing myself from the cords that fastened me, rolled over and over toward the fire, and after a short time burned them asunder. I rose on my feet; stretched my stiffened sinews; snatched up my rifle, and, for once in my life, spared that of Indians. I now recollect how desirous I once or twice felt to lay open the sculls of the wretches with my tomahawk; but when I again thought upon killing beings unprepared and unable to defend themselves, it looked like murder without need, and I gave up the idea.

"But, sir, I felt determined to mark the spot, and walking to a thrifty ash sapling, I cut out of it three large chips, and ran off. I soon reached the river; soon crossed it, and threw myself deep into the canebrakes, imitating the tracks of an Indian with my feet, so that no chance might be left for those from whom I had escaped to overtake me.

"It is now nearly twenty years since this happened, and more than five since I left the whites' settlements, which I might probably never have visited again, had I not been called on as a witness in a lawsuit that was pending in Kentucky and which, I really believe, would never [Pg 137] have been settled, had I not come forward, and established the beginning of a certain boundary line. This is the story, sir.

"Mr. —— moved from old Virginia into Kentucky, and having a large tract granted to him in the new state, laid claim to a certain parcel of land adjoining Green river, and as chance would have it, he took for one of his corners the very ash tree on which I had made my mark, and finished his survey of some thousands of acres, beginning, as it is expressed in the deed, 'at an ash marked by three distinct notches of the tomahawk of a white man.'

"The tree had grown much, and the bark had covered the marks; but, some how or other, Mr. —— heard from some one all that I have already said to you, and thinking that I might remember the spot alluded to in the deed, but which was no longer discoverable, wrote for me to come and try at least to find the place on the tree. His letter mentioned, that all my expenses should be paid; and not caring much about once more going back to Kentucky, I started and met Mr. ——. After some conversation, the affair with the Indians came to my recollection. I considered for a while, and began to think that after all, I could find the very spot, as well as the tree, if it was yet standing. [Pg 138]

"Mr. —— and I mounted our horses, and off we went to the Green river bottoms. After some difficulties, for you must be aware, sir, that great changes had taken place in these woods, I found at last the spot where I had crossed the river, and waiting for the moon to rise, made for the course in which I thought the ash tree grew. On approaching the place, I felt as if the Indians were there still, and as if I was still a prisoner among them. Mr. —— and I camped near what I conceived the spot, and waited till the return of day.

"At the rising of the sun I was on foot, and after a good deal of musing, thought that an ash tree then in sight must be the very one on which I had made my mark. I felt as if there could be no doubt of it, and mentioned my thought to Mr. ——. 'Well, Colonel Boone,' said he, 'if you think so, I hope it may prove true, but we must have some witnesses; do you stay hereabout, and I will go and bring some of the settlers whom I know.' I agreed. Mr. —— trotted off, and I, to pass the time, rambled about to see if a deer was still living in the land. But ah! sir, what a wonderful difference thirty years make in the country! Why, at the time when I was caught by the Indians, you would not have walked out in any direction for more than a mile without shooting a buck or a bear. There were ten thousands of buffaloes on the hills in Kentucky; the land looked [Pg 139] as if it would never become poor; and to hunt in those days was a pleasure indeed. But when I was left to myself on the banks of the Green river, I dare say for the last time in my life, a few *signs* only of deer were to be seen, and as to a deer itself, I saw none.

"Mr. —— returned, accompanied by three gentlemen. They looked upon me as if I had been Washington himself, and walked to the ash tree which I now called my own, as if in quest of a long lost treasure. I took an axe from one of them and cut a few chips off the bark. Still no signs were to be seen. So I cut again, until I thought it time to be cautious, and I scraped and worked away with my butcher knife, until I *did* come to where my tomahawk had left an impression in the wood. We now went regularly to work, and scraped at the tree with care, until three hacks, as plain as any three notches ever were, could be seen. Mr. —— and the other gentlemen were astonished, and, I must allow, I was as much surprised as pleased, myself. I made affidavit of this remarkable occurrence in the presence of these gentlemen. Mr. —— gained his cause. I left Green river, for ever, and came to where we now are; and, sir, I wish you a good night."

Here, too, it was that he resided, when Mr. Astor attempted to carry out his magnificent design, of settling Astoria on the western coast [Pg 140] of our continent, and belting the earth with his commerce. When you are older, you can read the beautiful history of that attempt, written by our distinguished countryman Mr. Irving. As the party, bound for the far west, moved up the Missouri, Boone stood upon the banks of the stream, looking anxiously after them. It was just the adventure to please him. There the old man stood, leaning upon his rifle, his dim eye lighted up as he gazed upon them, and his heart heavy with sorrow, because he was too old to press with them, beyond the mountains. [5]

Other sorrows than those of age, now crept upon him. His wife, who had been to him all that was good, was now taken from him, and the old man was left widowed. With a sad heart he now went to the home of his son, Major Nathan Boone.

The last war with England now broke out, too, and penetrated even the wilds of Missouri. It was the worst of all warfare—the savages were let loose upon them. Boone was too old to act the part of a soldier, but he sent off many substitutes in his sons.

When peace returned, the spirit of the old man rallied; his ruling passion was still with him. The woods were again his home, his rifle his companion; and thus he lived on, through a vigorous old age, with a passion as strong as ever, a hunter almost to the very day of his [Pg 141] death. For when, in 1818, death came upon him, he had but little notice of its approach. With no disease but old age, which had seemed comparatively vigorous almost to the day of his departure, he died in his eighty-fourth year. His mind was unclouded and he passed from this world calmly and quietly.

I have but one thing more to say. You remember Daniel Boone's schoolboy days, of which I have spoken. He left school a perfectly ignorant lad. Some say that he afterward learned to write, and produce as an evidence, a little narrative of his wanderings in Kentucky, supposed to be written by himself. I believe, however, that to the day of his death, he could not write his name. The narrative spoken of, was, I think, dictated in some degree by him, and written by another. At all events, the story is interesting and curious, and, as such, I have placed it for your benefit, as an appendix to this volume. [Pg 142] [Pg 143]

[1] This was the Indian name for the country.

[2] It is said by some that this man did not thus leave them. Their story is, that the three started out upon a hunt; that this man was separated from the Boones, and became entangled in a swamp. The Boones searched for him, but could not find him. Afterward, they found fragments of his clothes, which convinced them that the poor man had been torn to pieces by wolves.

Daniel Boone, however, tells a different story. He says that the man left them, "and returned home by himself;" and I have preferred his statement to any other.

[3] This mode of marking their track is often practised by hunters in the woods. As they pass through the forest, they mark the trees by cutting off a small piece of the bark. This enables them again to find the same pathway, and is commonly called "blazing the track."

[4] It is said that it was by Daniel Boone's advice that they first thought of making this purchase.

[5] See Irving's Astoria.

APPENDIX.

THE ADVENTURES OF COLONEL DANIEL BOONE,

FORMERLY A HUNTER;

CONTAINING A NARRATIVE OF THE WARS OF KENTUCKY,

AS GIVEN BY HIMSELF.

CURIOSITY is natural to the soul of man, and interesting objects have a powerful influence on our affections. Let these influencing powers actuate, by the permission or disposal of Providence, from selfish or social views, yet in time the mysterious will of Heaven is unfolded, and we behold our conduct, from whatsoever motives excited, operating to answer the important designs of Heaven. Thus we behold Kentucky, lately a howling wilderness, the habitation of savages and wild beasts, become a fruitful field; this region, so favorably distinguished by nature, now become the habitation of civilization, [Pg 144] at a period unparalleled in history, in the midst of a raging war, and under all the disadvantages of emigration to a country so remote from the inhabited parts of the continent. Here, where the hand of violence shed the blood of the innocent; where the horrid yells of savages and the groans of the distressed sounded in our ears, we now hear the praises and adorations of our Creator; where wretched wigwams stood, the miserable abodes of savages, we behold the foundations of cities laid, that, in all probability, will equal the glory of the greatest upon earth. And we view Kentucky, situated on the fertile banks of the great Ohio, rising from obscurity to shine with splendor equal to any other of the stars of the American hemisphere.

The settling of this region well deserves a place in history. Most of the memorable events I have myself been exercised in; and, for the satisfaction of the public, will briefly relate the circumstances of my adventures, and scenes of life, from my first movement to this country until this day.

It was on the first of May, in the year 1769, that I resigned my domestic happiness for a time, and left my family and peaceable habitation on the Yadkin river, in North Carolina, to wander through the wilderness of America, in quest of the country of Kentucky, in company with John Finley, John Stewart, Joseph Holden, James Monay, [Pg 145] and William Cool. We proceeded successfully, and after a long and fatiguing journey through a mountainous wilderness, in a westward direction, on the 7th day of June following we found ourselves on Red river, where John Finley had formerly been trading with the Indians, and, from the top of an eminence, saw with pleasure the beautiful level of Kentucky. Here let me observe that for some time we had experienced the most uncomfortable weather, as a prelibation of our future sufferings. At this place we encamped, and made a shelter to defend us from the inclement season, and began to hunt and reconnoitre the country. We found everywhere abundance of wild beasts of all sorts, through this vast forest. The buffalo were more frequent than I have seen cattle in the settlements, browsing on the leaves of the cane, or cropping the herbage on those extensive plains, fearless, because ignorant, of the violence of man. Sometimes we saw hundreds in a drove, and the numbers about the salt springs were amazing. In this forest, the habitation of beasts of every kind natural to America, we practised hunting with great success until the 22d day of December following.

This day John Stewart and I had a pleasing ramble, but fortune changed the scene in the close of it. We had passed through a great forest, [Pg 146] on which stood myriads of trees, some gay with blossoms, and others rich with fruits. Nature was here a series of wonders, and a fund of delight. Here she displayed her ingenuity and industry in a variety of flowers and fruits, beautifully colored, elegantly shaped, and charmingly flavored; and we were diverted with innumerable animals presenting themselves perpetually to our view. In the decline of the day, near Kentucky river, as we ascended the brow of a small hill, a number of Indians rushed out of a thick canebrake upon us, and made us prisoners. The time of our sorrow was now arrived, and the scene fully opened. The Indians plundered us of what we had, and kept us in confinement seven days, treating us with common savage usage. During this time we discovered no uneasiness or desire to escape, which made them less suspicious of us; but in the dead of night, as we lay in a thick canebrake by a large fire, when sleep had locked up their senses, my situation not disposing me for rest, I touched my companion, and gently awoke him. We improved this favorable opportunity, and departed, leaving them to take their rest, and speedily directed our course toward our old camp, but found it plundered, and the company dispersed and gone home. About this time my brother, Squire Boone, with another adventurer, who came to explore the country shortly after us, was wandering through the forest, [Pg 147] determined to find me if possible, and accidentally found our camp. Notwithstanding the unfortunate circumstances of our company, and our dangerous situation, as surrounded with hostile savages, our meeting so fortunately in the wilderness made us reciprocally sensible of the utmost satisfaction. So much does friendship triumph over misfortune, that sorrows and sufferings vanish at the meeting not only of real friends, but of the most distant acquaintances, and substitute happiness in their room.

Soon after this, my companion in captivity, John Stewart, was killed by the savages, and the man that came with my brother returned home by himself. We were then in a dangerous, helpless situation, exposed daily to perils and death among savages and wild beasts—not a white man in the country but ourselves.

Thus situated, many hundred miles from our families in the howling wilderness, I believe few would have equally enjoyed the happiness we experienced. I often observed to my brother, "You see now how little nature requires, to be satisfied. Felicity, the companion of content, is rather found in our own breasts than in the enjoyment of external things; and I firmly believe it requires but a little philosophy to make a man happy in whatsoever state he is. This consists in a full resignation to the will of Providence; and a resigned soul finds [Pg 148] pleasure in a path strewed with briers and thorns."

We continued not in a state of indolence, but hunted every day, and prepared a little cottage to defend us from the winter storms. We remained there undisturbed during the winter; and on the 1st day of May, 1770, my brother returned home to the settlement by himself, for a new recruit of horses and ammunition, leaving me by myself, without bread, salt, or sugar, without company of my fellow-creatures, or even a horse or dog. I confess I never before was under greater necessity of exercising philosophy and fortitude. A few days I passed uncomfortably. The idea of a beloved wife and family, and their anxiety upon the account of my absence and exposed situation, made sensible impressions on my heart. A thousand dreadful apprehensions presented themselves to my view, and had undoubtedly disposed me to melancholy, if further indulged.

One day I undertook a tour through the country, and the diversity and beauties of nature I met with in this charming season, expelled every gloomy and vexatious thought. Just at the close of day the gentle gales retired, and left the place to the disposal of a profound calm. Not a breeze shook the most tremulous leaf. I had gained the summit of a commanding ridge, and, looking round with astonishing delight, beheld the ample plains, the beauteous tracts below. On the other [Pg 149] hand, I surveyed the famous river Ohio that rolled in silent dignity, marking the western boundary of

Kentucky with inconceivable grandeur. At a vast distance I beheld the mountains lift their venerable brows, and penetrate the clouds. All things were still. I kindled a fire near a fountain of sweet water, and feasted on the loin of a buck, which a few hours before I had killed. The sullen shades of night soon overspread the whole hemisphere, and the earth seemed to gasp after the hovering moisture. My roving excursion this day had fatigued my body, and diverted my imagination. I laid me down to sleep, and I awoke not until the sun had chased away the night. I continued this tour, and in a few days explored a considerable part of the country, each day equally pleased as the first. I returned again to my old camp, which was not disturbed in my absence. I did not confine my lodging to it, but often reposed in thick canebrakes, to avoid the savages, who, I believe, often visited my camp, but, fortunately for me, in my absence. In this situation I was constantly exposed to danger and death. How unhappy such a situation for a man tormented with fear, which is vain if no danger comes, and if it does, only augments the pain! It was my happiness to be destitute of this afflicting passion, with which I had the greatest reason to be [Pg 150] affected. The prowling wolves diverted my nocturnal hours with perpetual howlings; and the various species of animals in this vast forest, in the daytime, were continually in my view.

Thus I was surrounded by plenty in the midst of want. I was happy in the midst of dangers and inconveniences. In such a diversity, it was impossible I should be disposed to melancholy. No populous city, with all the varieties of commerce and stately structures, could afford so much pleasure to my mind as the beauties of nature I found here.

Thus, through an uninterrupted scene of sylvan pleasures, I spent the time until the 27th day of July following, when my brother, to my great felicity, met me, according to appointment, at our old camp. Shortly after, we left this place, not thinking it safe to stay there longer, and proceeded to Cumberland river, reconnoitring that part of the country until March, 1771, and giving names to the different waters.

Soon after, I returned home to my family, with a determination to bring them as soon as possible to live in Kentucky, which I esteemed a second paradise, at the risk of my life and fortune.

I returned safe to my old habitation, and found my family in happy circumstances. I sold my farm on the Yadkin, and what goods we could not carry with us; and on the 25th day of September, [Pg 151] 1773, bade a farewell to our friends, and proceeded on our journey to Kentucky, in company with five families more, and forty men that joined us in Powel's Valley, which is one hundred and fifty miles from the now settled parts of Kentucky. This promising beginning was soon overcast with a cloud of adversity; for, upon the 10th day of October, the rear of our company was attacked by a number of Indians, who killed six, and wounded one man. Of these, my eldest son was one that fell in the action. Though we defended ourselves, and repulsed the enemy, yet this unhappy affair scattered out cattle, brought us into extreme difficulty, and so discouraged the whole company, that we retreated forty miles, to the settlement on Clinch river. We had passed over two mountains, viz., Powel's and Walden's, and were approaching Cumberland mountain when this adverse fortune overtook us. These mountains are in the wilderness, as we pass from the old settlements in Virginia to Kentucky, are ranged in a southwest and northeast direction, are of a great length and breadth, and not far distant from each other. Over these, nature hath formed passes that are less difficult than might be expected, from a view of such huge piles. The aspect of these cliffs is so wild and horrid, that it is impossible to behold them without terror. The spectator is apt to imagine that nature had formerly suffered [Pg 152] some violent convulsion, and that these are the dismembered remains of the dreadful shock: the ruins, not of Persepolis or Palmyra, but of the world!

I remained with my family on Clinch until the 6th of June, 1774, when I and one Michael Stoner were solicited by Governor Dunmore of Virginia to go to the falls of the Ohio, to conduct into the settlement a number of surveyors that had been sent thither by him some months before; this country having about this time drawn the attention of many adventurers. We immediately complied with the Governor's request, and conducted in the surveyors—completing a tour of eight hundred miles, through many difficulties, in sixty-two days.

Soon after I returned home, I was ordered to take the command of three garrisons during the campaign which Governor Dunmore carried on against the Shawanese Indians; after the conclusion of which, the militia was discharged from each garrison, and I, being relieved from my post, was solicited by a number of North Carolina gentlemen, that were about purchasing the lands lying on the south side of Kentucky river, from the Cherokee Indians, to attend their treaty at Wataga in March, 1775, to negotiate with them, and mention the boundaries of the purchase. This I accepted; and, at the request of the same gentlemen, [Pg 153] undertook to mark out a road in the best passage from the settlement through the wilderness to Kentucky, with such assistance as I thought necessary to employ for such an important undertaking.

I soon began this work, having collected a number of enterprising men, well armed. We proceeded with all possible expedition until we came within fifteen miles of where Boonesborough now stands, and where we were fired upon by a party of Indians that killed two, and wounded two of our number; yet, although surprised and taken at a disadvantage, we stood our ground. This was on the 20th of March, 1775. Three days after, we were fired upon again, and had two men killed, and three wounded. Afterward we proceeded on to Kentucky river without opposition; and on the 1st day of April began to erect the fort of Boonesborough at a salt lick, about sixty yards from the river, on the south side.

On the fourth day, the Indians killed one of our men. We were busily employed in building this fort until the 14th day of June following, without any further opposition from the Indians; and having finished the works, I returned to my family, on Clinch.

In a short time I proceeded to remove my family from Clinch to this garrison, where we arrived safe, without any other difficulties than [Pg 154] such as are common to this passage; my wife and daughter being the first white women that ever stood on the banks of Kentucky river.

On the 24th day of December following, we had one man killed, and one wounded, by the Indians, who seemed determined to persecute us for erecting this fortification.

On the 14th day of July, 1776, two of Colonel Calaway's daughters, and one of mine, were taken prisoners near the fort. I immediately pursued the Indians with only eight men, and on the 16th overtook them, killed two of the party, and recovered the girls. The same day on which this attempt was made, the Indians divided themselves into different parties, and attacked several forts, which were shortly before this time erected, doing a great deal of mischief. This was extremely distressing to the new settlers. The innocent husbandman was shot down, while busy in cultivating the soil for his family's supply. Most of the cattle around the stations were destroyed. They continued their hostilities in this manner until the 15th of April, 1777, when they attacked Boonesborough with a party of above one hundred in number, killed one man, and wounded four. Their loss in this attack was not certainly known to us.

On the 4th day of July following, a party of about two hundred Indians attacked Boonesborough, [Pg 155] killed one man, and wounded two. They besieged us forty-eight hours, during which time seven of them were killed, and, at last, finding themselves not likely to prevail, they raised the siege, and departed.

The Indians had disposed their warriors in different parties at this time, and attacked the different garrisons, to prevent their assisting each other, and did much injury to the distressed inhabitants.

On the 19th day of this month, Colonel Logan's fort was besieged by a party of about two hundred Indians. During this dreadful siege they did a great deal of mischief, distressed the garrison, in which were only fifteen men, killed two, and wounded one. The enemy's loss was uncertain, from the common practice which the Indians have of carrying off their dead in time of battle. Colonel Harrod's fort was then defended by only sixty-five men, and Boonesborough by twenty-two, there being no more forts or white men in the country, except at the Falls, a considerable distance from these: and all, taken collectively, were but a handful to the numerous warriors that were everywhere dispersed through the country, intent upon doing all the mischief that savage barbarity could invent. Thus we passed through a scene of sufferings that exceeds description.

On the 25th of this month, a reinforcement of [Pg 156] forty-five men arrived from North Carolina, and about the 20th of August following, Colonel Bowman arrived with one hundred men from Virginia. Now we began to strengthen; and hence, for the space of six weeks, we had skirmishes with Indians, in one quarter or other, almost every day.

The savages now learned the superiority of the Long Knife, as they call the Virginians, by experience; being outgeneralled in almost every battle. Our affairs began to wear a new aspect, and the enemy, not daring to venture on open war, practised secret mischief at times.

On the 1st day of January, 1778, I went with a party of thirty men to the Blue Licks, on Licking river, to make salt for the different garrisons in the country.

On the 7th day of February, as I was hunting to procure meat for the company, I met with a party of one hundred and two Indians, and two Frenchmen, on their march against Boonesborough, that place being particularly the object of the enemy.

They pursued, and took me; and brought me on the 8th day to the Licks, where twenty-seven of my party were, three of them having previously returned home with the salt. I, knowing it was impossible for them to escape, capitulated with the enemy, and, at a distance, in their view, [Pg 157] gave notice to my men of their situation, with orders not to resist, but surrender themselves captives.

The generous usage the Indians had promised before in my capitulation, was afterward fully complied with, and we proceeded with them as prisoners to Old Chilicothe, the principal Indian town on Little Miami, where we arrived, after an uncomfortable journey in very severe weather, on the 18th day of February, and received as good treatment as prisoners could expect from savages. On the 10th day of March following, I and ten of my men were conducted by forty Indians to Detroit, where we arrived the 30th day, and were treated by Governor Hamilton, the British commander at that post, with great humanity.

During our travels, the Indians entertained me well, and their affection for me was so great, that they utterly refused to leave me there with the others, although the Governor offered them one hundred pounds sterling for me, on purpose to give me a parole to go home. Several English gentlemen there, being sensible of my adverse fortune, and touched with human sympathy, generously offered a friendly supply for my wants, which I refused, with many thanks for their kindness—adding, that I never expected it would be in my power to recompense such unmerited generosity. [Pg 158]

The Indians left my men in captivity with the British at Detroit, and on the 10th day of April brought me toward Old Chilicothe, where we arrived on the 25th day of the same month. This was a long and fatiguing march, through an exceeding fertile country, remarkable for fine springs and streams of water. At Chilicothe I spent my time as comfortably as I could expect; was adopted, according to their custom, into a family, where I became a son, and had a great share in the affection of my new parents, brothers, sisters, and friends. I was exceedingly familiar and friendly with them, always appearing as cheerful and satisfied as possible, and they put great confidence in me. I often went a hunting with them, and frequently gained their applause for my activity at our shooting-matches. I was careful not to exceed many of them in shooting; for no people are more envious than they in this sport. I could observe, in their countenances and gestures, the greatest expressions of joy when they exceeded me; and, when the reverse happened, of envy. The Shawanese king took great notice of me, and treated me with profound respect and entire friendship, often intrusting me to hunt at my liberty. I frequently returned with the spoils of the woods, and as often presented some of what I had taken to him, expressive of duty to my sovereign. My food and lodging were in common with them; not so good, indeed, as I could [Pg 159] desire, but necessity made everything acceptable.

I now began to meditate an escape, and carefully avoided their suspicions, continuing with them at Old Chilicothe until the 1st day of June following, and then was taken by them to the salt springs on Scioto, and kept there making salt ten days. During this time I hunted some for them, and found the land, for a great extent about this river, to exceed the soil of Kentucky, if possible, and remarkably well watered.

When I returned to Chilicothe, alarmed to see four hundred and fifty Indians, of their choicest warriors, painted and armed in a fearful manner, ready to march against Boonesborough, I determined to escape the first opportunity.

On the 16th, before sunrise, I departed in the most secret manner, and arrived at Boonesborough on the 20th, after a journey of one hundred and sixty miles, during which I had but one meal.

I found our fortress in a bad state of defence; but we proceeded immediately to repair our flanks, strengthen our gates and posterns, and form double bastions, which we completed in ten days. In this time we daily expected the arrival of the Indian army; and at length, one of my fellow-prisoners, escaping from them, arrived, informing us that the enemy had, on account of my departure, [Pg 160] postponed their expedition three weeks. The Indians had spies out viewing our movements, and were greatly alarmed with our increase in number and fortifications. The grand councils of the nations were held frequently, and with more deliberation than usual. They evidently saw the approaching hour when the Long Knife would dispossess them of their desirable habitations; and, anxiously concerned for futurity, determined utterly to extirpate the whites out of Kentucky. We were not intimidated by their movements, but frequently gave them proofs of our courage.

About the first of August, I made an incursion into the Indian country with a party of nineteen men, in order to surprise a small town up Scioto, called Paint Creek Town. We advanced within four miles thereof, where we met a party of thirty Indians on their march against Boonesborough, intending to join the others from Chilicothe. A smart fight ensued between us for some time; at length the savages gave way and fled. We had no loss on our side; the enemy had one killed, and two wounded. We took from them three horses, and all their baggage; and being informed, by two of our number that went to their town, that the Indians had entirely evacuated it, we proceeded no further, and returned with all possible expedition to assist our garrison against the other party. We passed by them on the sixth day, [Pg 161] and on the seventh we arrived safe at Boonesborough.

On the 8th, the Indian army arrived, being four hundred and forty-four in number, commanded by Captain Duquesne, eleven other Frenchmen, and some of their own chiefs, and marched up within view of our fort, with British and French colors flying; and having sent a summons to me, in his Britannic Majesty's name, to surrender the fort, I requested two days' consideration, which was granted.

It was now a critical period with us. We were a small number in the garrison—a powerful army before our walls, whose appearance proclaimed inevitable death, fearfully painted, and marking their footsteps with desolation. Death was preferable to captivity; and if taken by storm, we must inevitably be devoted to destruction. In this situation we concluded to maintain our garrison, if possible. We immediately proceeded to collect what we could of our horses and other cattle, and bring them through the posterns into the fort; and in the evening of the 9th, I returned answer that we were determined to defend our fort while a man was living. "Now," said I to their commander, who stood attentively hearing my sentiments, "we laugh at your formidable preparations; but thank you for giving us notice and time to provide for our defence. Your efforts will not prevail; for [Pg 162] our gates shall for ever deny you admittance." Whether this answer affected their courage or not I can not tell; but, contrary to our expectations, they formed a scheme to deceive us, declaring it was their orders, from Governor Hamilton, to take us captives, and not to destroy us; but if nine of us would come out, and treat with them, they would immediately withdraw their forces from our walls, and return home peaceably. This sounded grateful in our ears; and we agreed to the proposal.

We held the treaty within sixty yards of the garrison, on purpose to divert them from a breach of honor, as we could not avoid suspicions of the savages. In this situation the articles were formally agreed to, and signed; and the Indians told us it was customary with them on such occasions for two Indians to shake hands with every white man in the treaty, as an evidence of entire friendship. We agreed to this also, but were soon convinced their policy was to take us prisoners. They immediately grappled us; but, although surrounded by hundreds of savages, we extricated ourselves from them, and escaped all safe into the garrison, except one that was wounded, through a heavy fire from their army. They immediately attacked us on every side, and a constant heavy fire ensued between us, day and night, for the space of nine days. [Pg 163]

In this time the enemy began to undermine our fort, which was situated sixty yards from Kentucky river. They began at the watermark, and proceeded in the bank some distance, which we understood, by their making the water muddy with the clay; and we immediately proceeded to disappoint their design, by cutting a trench across their subterranean passage. The enemy, discovering our counter-mine, by the clay we threw out of the fort, desisted from that stratagem: and experience now fully convincing them that neither their power nor policy could effect their purpose, on the 20th day of August they raised the siege and departed.

During this siege, which threatened death in every form, we had two men killed, and four wounded, besides a number of cattle. We killed of the enemy thirty-seven, and wounded a great number. After they were gone, we picked up one hundred and twenty-five pounds weight of bullets, besides what stuck in the logs of our fort, which certainly is a great proof of their industry. Soon after this, I went into the settlement, and nothing worthy of a place in this account passed in my affairs for some time.

During my absence from Kentucky, Colonel Bowman carried on an expedition against the Shawanese, at Old Chilicothe, with one hundred and sixty men, in July, 1779. Here they arrived undiscovered, and a [Pg 164] battle ensued, which lasted until ten o'clock, A.M., when Colonel Bowman, finding he could not succeed at this time, retreated about thirty miles. The Indians, in the mean time, collecting all their forces, pursued and overtook him, when a smart fight continued near two hours, not to the advantage of Colonel Bowman's party.

Colonel Harrod proposed to mount a number of horse, and furiously to rush upon the savages, who at this time fought with remarkable fury. This desperate step had a happy effect, broke their line of battle, and the savages fled on all sides. In these two battles we had nine killed, and one wounded. The enemy's loss uncertain, only two scalps being taken.

On the 22d day of June, 1780, a large party of Indians and Canadians, about six hundred in number, commanded by Colonel Bird, attacked Riddle's and Martin's stations, at the forks of Licking river, with six pieces of artillery. They carried this expedition so secretly, that the unwary inhabitants did not discover them until they fired upon the forts; and, not being prepared to oppose them, were obliged to surrender themselves miserable captives to barbarous savages, who immediately after tomahawked one man and two women, and loaded all the others with heavy baggage, forcing them along toward their towns, able [Pg 165] or unable to march. Such as were weak and faint by the way, they tomahawked. The tender women and helpless children fell victims to their cruelty. This, and the savage treatment they received afterward, is shocking to humanity, and too barbarous to relate.

The hostile disposition of the savages and their allies caused General Clarke, the commandant at the Falls of the Ohio, immediately to begin an expedition with his own regiment, and the armed force of the country, against Pecaway, the principal town of the Shawanese, on a branch of Great Miami, which he finished with great success, took seventeen scalps, and burnt the town to ashes, with the loss of seventeen men.

About this time I returned to Kentucky with my family; and here, to avoid an inquiry into my conduct, the reader being before informed of my bringing my family to Kentucky, I am under the necessity of informing him that, during my captivity with the Indians, my wife, who despaired of ever seeing me again—expecting the Indians had put a period to my life, oppressed with the distresses of the country, and bereaved of me, her only happiness—had, before I returned, transported my family and goods, on horses, through the wilderness, amid a multitude of dangers, to her father's house in North Carolina.

Shortly after the troubles at Boonesborough, I went to them, and [Pg 166] lived peaceably there until this time. The history of my going home, and returning with my family, forms a series of difficulties, an account of which would swell a volume; and, being foreign to my purpose, I shall purposely omit them.

I settled my family in Boonesborough once more; and shortly after, on the 6th day of October, 1780, I went in company with my brother to the Blue Licks; and, on our return home, we were fired upon by a party of Indians. They shot him, and pursued me, by the scent of their dog, three miles; but I killed the dog, and escaped. The winter soon came on, and was very severe, which confined the Indians to their wigwams.

The severity of this winter caused great difficulties in Kentucky. The enemy had destroyed most of the corn the summer before. This necessary article was scarce and dear, and the inhabitants lived chiefly on the flesh of buffalo. The circumstances of many were very lamentable: however, being a hardy race of people, and accustomed to difficulties and necessities, they were wonderfully supported through all their sufferings, until the ensuing autumn, when we received abundance from the fertile soil.

Toward spring we were frequently harassed by Indians; and in May, 1782, a party assaulted Ashton's station, killed one man, and took a [Pg 167] negro prisoner. Captain Ashton, with twenty-five men, pursued and overtook the savages, and a smart fight ensued, which lasted two hours; but they, being superior in number, obliged Captain Ashton's party to retreat, with the loss of eight killed, and four mortally wounded; their brave commander himself being numbered among the dead.

The Indians continued their hostilities; and, about the 10th of August following, two boys were taken from Major Hoy's station. This party was pursued by Captain Holder and seventeen men, who were also defeated, with the loss of four men killed, and one wounded. Our affairs became more and more alarming. Several stations which had lately been erected in the country were continually infested with savages, stealing their horses and killing the men at every opportunity. In a field, near Lexington, an Indian shot a man, and running to scalp him, was himself shot from the fort, and fell dead upon his enemy.

Every day we experienced recent mischiefs. The barbarous savage nations of Shawanese, Cherokees, Wyandots, Tawas, Delawares, and several others near Detroit, united in a war against us, and assembled their choicest warriors at Old Chilicothe, to go on the expedition, in order to destroy us, and entirely depopulate the country. Their savage minds were inflamed to mischief by two abandoned men, Captains M'Kee [Pg 168] and Girty. These led them to execute every diabolical scheme, and on the 15th day of August, commanded a party of Indians and Canadians, of about five hundred in number, against Bryant's station, five miles from Lexington. Without demanding a surrender, they furiously assaulted the garrison, which was happily prepared to oppose them; and, after they had expended much ammunition in vain, and killed the cattle round the fort, not being likely to make themselves masters of this place, they raised the siege, and departed in the morning of the third day after they came, with the loss of about thirty killed, and the number of wounded uncertain. Of the garrison, four were killed, and three wounded.

On the 18th day, Colonel Todd, Colonel Trigg, Major Harland, and myself, speedily collected one hundred and seventy-six men, well armed, and pursued the savages. They had marched beyond the Blue Licks, to a remarkable bend of the main fork of Licking river, about forty-three miles from Lexington, where we overtook them on the 19th day. The savages observing us, gave way; and we, being ignorant of their numbers, passed the river. When the enemy saw our proceedings, having greatly the advantage of us in situation, they formed the line of battle, from one bend of Licking to the other, about a mile from [Pg 169] the Blue Licks. An exceeding fierce battle immediately began, for about fifteen minutes, when we, being overpowered by numbers, were obliged to retreat, with the loss of sixty-seven men, seven of whom were taken prisoners. The brave and much-lamented Colonels Todd and Trigg, Major Harland, and my second son, were among the dead. We were informed that the Indians, numbering their dead, found they had four killed more than we; and therefore four of the prisoners they had taken were, by general consent, ordered to be killed in a most barbarous manner by the young warriors, in order to train them up to cruelty; and then they proceeded to their towns.

On our retreat we were met by Colonel Logan, hastening to join us, with a number of well-armed men. This powerful assistance we unfortunately wanted in the battle; for, notwithstanding the enemy's superiority of numbers, they acknowledged, that, if they had received one more fire from us, they should undoubtedly have given way. So valiantly did our small party fight, that, to the memory of those who unfortunately fell in the battle, enough of honor can not be paid. Had Colonel Logan and his party been with us, it is highly probable we should have given the savages a total defeat.

I can not reflect upon this dreadful scene, but sorrow fills my [Pg 170] heart. A zeal for the defence of their country led these heroes to the scene of action, though with a few men to attack a powerful army of experienced warriors. When we gave way, they pursued us with the utmost eagerness, and in every quarter spread destruction. The river was difficult to cross, and many were killed in the flight—some just entering the river, some in the water, others after crossing, in ascending the cliffs. Some escaped on horseback, a few on foot; and, being dispersed everywhere in a few hours, brought the melancholy news of this unfortunate battle to Lexington. Many widows were now made. The reader may guess what sorrow filled the hearts of the inhabitants, exceeding anything that I am able to describe. Being reinforced, we returned to bury the dead, and found their bodies strewed everywhere, cut and mangled in a dreadful manner. This mournful scene exhibited a horror almost unparalleled: some torn and eaten by wild beasts; those in the river eaten by fishes; all in such a putrefied condition, that no one could be distinguished from another.

As soon as General Clarke, then at the Falls of the Ohio—who was ever our ready friend, and merits the love and gratitude of all his countrymen—understood the circumstances of this unfortunate action, he ordered an expedition, with all possible haste, to pursue the [Pg 171] savages, which was so expeditiously effected, that we overtook them within two miles of their towns: and probably might have obtained a great victory, had not two of their number met us about two hundred poles before we came up. These returned quick as lightning to their camp, with the alarming news of a mighty army in view. The savages fled in the utmost disorder, evacuated their towns, and reluctantly left their territory to our mercy. We immediately took possession of Old Chilicothe without opposition, being deserted by its inhabitants. We continued our pursuit through five towns on the Miami rivers, Old Chilicothe, Pecaway, New Chilicothe, Will's Towns, and Chilicothe—burnt them all to ashes, entirely destroyed their corn, and other fruits, and everywhere spread a scene of desolation in the country. In this expedition we took seven prisoners and five scalps, with the loss of only four men, two of whom were accidentally killed by our own army.

This campaign in some measure damped the spirits of the Indians, and made them sensible of our superiority. Their connexions were dissolved, their armies scattered, and a future invasion put entirely out of their power; yet they continued to practise mischief secretly upon the inhabitants, in the exposed parts of the country. [Pg 172]

In October following, a party made an excursion into that district called the Crab Orchard; and one of them, being advanced some distance before the others, boldly entered the house of a poor defenceless family, in which was only a negro man, a woman, and her children, terrified with the apprehensions of immediate death. The savage, perceiving their defenceless situation, without offering violence to the family, attempted to capture the negro, who happily proved an overmatch for him, threw him on the ground, and, in the struggle, the mother of the children drew an axe from a corner of the cottage, and cut his head off, while her little daughter shut the door. The savages instantly appeared, and applied their tomahawks to the door. An old rusty gun-barrel, without a lock, lay in a corner, which the mother put through a small crevice, and the savages, perceiving it, fled. In the mean time, the alarm spread through the neighborhood; the armed men collected immediately, and pursued the ravagers into the wilderness. Thus Providence, by the means of this negro, saved the whole of the poor family from destruction. From that time until the happy return of peace between the United States and Great Britain, the Indians did us no mischief. Finding the great king beyond the water disappointed in his expectations, and conscious of the importance of the Long Knife, and their own wretchedness, some of the nations [Pg 173] immediately desired peace; to which, at present [1784], they seem universally disposed, and are sending ambassadors to General Clarke, at the Falls of the Ohio, with the minutes of their councils.

To conclude, I can now say that I have verified the saying of an old Indian who signed Colonel Henderson's deed. Taking me by the hand, at the delivery thereof—"Brother," said he, "we have given you a fine land, but I believe you will have much trouble in settling it." My footsteps have often been marked with blood, and therefore I can truly subscribe to its original name. Two darling sons and a brother have I lost by savage hands, which have also taken from me forty valuable horses, and abundance of cattle. Many dark and sleepless nights have I been a companion for owls, separated from the cheerful society of men, scorched by the summer's sun, and pinched by the winter's cold—an instrument ordained to settle the wilderness. But now the scene is changed: peace crowns the sylvan shade.

What thanks, what ardent and ceaseless thanks are due to that all-superintending Providence which has turned a cruel war into peace, brought order out of confusion, made the fierce savages placid, and turned away their hostile weapons from our country! May the same Almighty Goodness banish the accursed monster, war, from all lands, [Pg 174] with her hated associates, rapine and insatiable ambition! Let peace, descending from her native heaven, bid her olives spring amid the joyful nations; and plenty, in league with commerce, scatter blessings from her copious hand!

This account of my adventures will inform the reader of the most remarkable events of this country. I now live in peace and safety, enjoying the sweets of liberty, and the bounties of Providence, with my once fellow-sufferers, in this delightful country, which I have seen purchased with a vast expense of blood and treasure: delighting in the prospect of its being, in a short time, one of the most opulent and powerful states on the continent of North America; which, with the love and gratitude of my countrymen, I esteem a sufficient reward for all my toil and dangers.

DANIEL BOONE.
Fayette County, Kentucky.

THE END.